### Book Three

## Program Authors

**Linda Ward Beech • James Beers • Jo Ann Dauzat
Sam V. Dauzat • Tara McCarthy**

## Program Consultants

Myra K. Baum
Office of Adult and
   Continuing Education
Brooklyn, New York

Francis J. Feltman, Jr.
Racine Youth Offender
   Correctional Facility
Racine, Wisconsin

Mary Ann Guilliams
Gary Job Corps
San Marcos, Texas

Julie Jacobs
Inmate Literacy Project
Santa Clara County Library
Milpitas, California

Maxine L. McCormick
Workforce Education
Orange County Public Schools
Orlando, Florida

Sandra S. Owens
Laurens County Literacy Council
Laurens, South Carolina

www.steck-vaughn.com

# Acknowledgments

## Staff Credits
**Executive Editor:** Ellen Northcutt
**Senior Editor:** Donna Townsend
**Associate Design Director:** Joyce Spicer
**Supervising Designer:** Pamela Heaney
**Designer:** Jessica Bristow
**Production Coordinator:** Rebecca Gonzales
**Electronic Production Artist:** Julia Miracle-Hagaman
**Senior Technical Advisor:** Alan Klemp
**Electronic Production Specialist:** Dina Bahan

## Photography Credits
Cover (man with guitar) Christine Galida; (mother and son) Park Street; (people at table) Tomás Ovalle; (woman and dog) Ken Walker; pp.2, 12-13 Christine Galida; pp.16, 26-27 Park Street; pp.30, 40-42 Christine Galida; pp.44, 54-55 Ken Lax; pp.58, 68-69 Ken Walker; pp.72, 82-83, Park Street; pp.86, 96-97 Tomás Ovalle. Additional photography by: ©Photodisc

## Literary Credits
"Until I Saw the Sea" from *I Feel the Same Way* by Lilian Moore. Copyright © 1967, 1995 by Lilian Moore. Used by permission of Marian Reiner for the author.

**ISBN 0-7398-2841-X**

Copyright © 2001 Steck-Vaughn Company
All rights reserved. No part of the material protected by this copyright may be reproduced or utilized in any form or by any means, electronic or mechanical, including photocopying, recording, or by any information storage and retrieval system, without permission in writing from the copyright owner. Requests for permission to make copies of any part of the work should be mailed to:
Copyright Permissions, Steck-Vaughn Company, P.O. Box 26015, Austin, Texas 78755.

Printed in the United States of America

# Contents

To the Learner ..................................1

## Unit 1

### Finding Ways to Increase Income

Story 1: A Plan to Save the Store ......3
Review Words..................................4
Sight Words ....................................5
Phonics: Short *e* (-ell) ......................8
Phonics: Long *a* (-ake) .....................9
Writing Skills:
   Compound Words ........................10
Comprehension:
   Think and Write ...........................14
Unit 1 Review ................................15

## Unit 2

### Rearing Children

Story 2: Looking Out for Me ...........17
Review Words.................................18
Sight Words ...................................19
Phonics: Short *u* (-ug) ....................22
Phonics: Long *i* (-ine) .....................23
Writing Skills:
   Irregular Plurals...........................24
Comprehension:
   Think and Write ...........................28
Unit 2 Review ................................29

## Unit 3

### Promoting Health Care

Story 3: In Good Health ..................31
Review Words.................................32
Sight Words ...................................33
Phonics: Short *i* (-ip) ......................36
Phonics: Long *o* (-ope) ...................37
Writing Skills:
   Adding *-er* to Naming Words .........38
Comprehension:
   Think and Write ...........................42
Unit 3 Review ................................43

## Unit 4

### Handling Social Relationships

Story 4: A Team at Work ................45
Review Words.................................46
Sight Words ...................................47
Phonics: Long *a* (-ay) .....................50
Phonics: Long *e* (-eed) ...................51
Writing Skills:
   Using Commas ............................52
Comprehension:
   Think and Write ...........................56
Unit 4 Review ................................57

## Unit 5

### Learning About Training Programs

Story 5: Helping Dogs to Help People .59

Review Words ................................... 60

Sight Words ...................................... 61

Phonics: Long *i (-ight)* ..................... 64

Phonics: Long *u (-une, -ute)* ........... 65

Writing Skills:
  Irregular Verbs .............................. 66

Comprehension:
  Think and Write ............................ 70

Unit 5 Review .................................. 71

## Unit 6

### Coping with Job Dissatisfaction

Story 6: A Life on the Go ................ 73

Review Words ................................... 74

Sight Words ...................................... 75

Phonics: Short *i (-ig)* ...................... 78

Phonics: Long *o (-old)* .................... 79

Writing Skills:
  Dropping Final *e* to Add *-ed*
  and *-ing* ..................................... 80

Comprehension:
  Think and Write ............................ 84

Unit 6 Review .................................. 85

## Unit 7

### Working Together for Change

Story 7: The Plan That Grew ........... 87

Review Words ................................... 88

Sight Words ...................................... 89

Phonics: Short *a (-ag)* ..................... 92

Phonics: Long *e (-eat)* .................... 93

Writing Skills:
  Quotation Marks ........................... 94

Comprehension:
  Think and Write ............................ 98

Unit 7 Review .................................. 99

At Your Leisure ............................... 100

Final Review .................................. 102

Answer Key .................................... 106

Learner Checklist ........................... 121

Word List ....................................... 122

Learner Placement Form ............ Inside Back Cover

## To the Learner

In this book, you will read interesting stories and see your reading skills grow. The book has seven units. Each unit has a story about a different life skill. As you read the stories, you will review words you already know and learn new words. You will also learn and practice a writing skill. Then you will review the skills you have learned before you move on to the next unit.

At the end of the book, in the At Your Leisure section, you will have a chance to read just for fun. This section has a poem and another reading selection for you to enjoy.

Have a good time using this book. It is written for you!

**Instructor's Notes:** Read this page with students. Discuss having students keep a notebook or journal of words and original sentences they write. Refer to the *Reading for Today Instructor's Guide* for lesson plans, optional teaching activities, and a discussion of how to use the Learner Placement Form on the inside back cover of this book.

# Unit 1   Finding Ways to Increase Income

## Discussion

**Remember**

Look at the picture. Have you ever been to a music store like this?

**Predict**

Look at the picture and the story title. What do you think this story is about?

# A Plan to Save the Store

My brother Max has a music store. He likes the work and the people who stop in. Max loves guitars. His friends say he is good at fixing old guitars. I'd like to have a job I can love like Max loves his.

At one time the money Max got from the music store was good. But times are not the same. People do stop by the store, but they don't buy like they did. Max is in big trouble. Is it time for him to quit? Or can I help Max make a plan to save the store?

*The story continues.*

## Review Words

**A. Check the words you know.**

☐ 1. plan   ☐ 2. goods   ☐ 3. guitars

☐ 4. quit   ☐ 5. lose   ☐ 6. old

☐ 7. music   ☐ 8. won't   ☐ 9. some

☐ 10. time   ☐ 11. help   ☐ 12. trouble

**B. Read and write the sentences. Circle all the review words.**

1. Max has ⓣrouble with his ⓜusic store.
   _____

2. Some of the goods in the store are old.
   _____

3. Max likes to fix old guitars.
   _____

4. Max won't quit, but it's time for him to get some help.
   _____

5. Will Max find a plan, or will he lose money?
   _____

**C. Write a sentence. Use a review word.**

_____

**Instructor's Notes:** Read each set of directions with students. For A, have students read the words aloud and then check known words. In B, explain the meaning of *goods* in this context: "wares" or "merchandise." For C, point out the icon in the margin and tell students it indicates a place for them to produce their own writing.

# Sight Words

see • tapes • sell

**A. Read the words above. Then read the sentence.**

I **see** that Max has no music **tapes** to **sell**.

**B. Underline the new words in sentences 1–4.**

1. When people stop by the store, they don't see tapes for sale.

2. Max can sell tapes in his music store.

3. He can make bigger sales with tapes.

4. Will Max see that tapes can help the store?

**C. Write the three new words into the puzzle.**

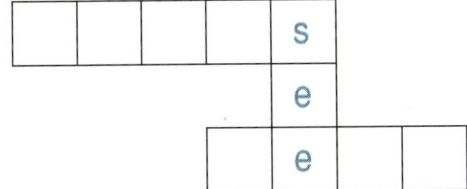

**D. Write the word that best completes each sentence.**

    sell    tape    see

1. Goods that are out of date don't _____ .

2. People like to buy music on _____ .

3. Will Max _____ that my plan will make money?

 **E. Write your own sentence. Use one of the new words.**

_____

**Instructor's Notes:** Read each set of directions with students. Read each sight word aloud. Have students repeat. Discuss the difference between the words *sell* and *sale*.

take • records • shop

**A. Read the words above. Then read the sentence.**

Take the records out of the shop.

**B. Underline the new words in sentences 1–4.**

1. Max has a lot of old records in the shop.

2. We can sell the records for a quarter.

3. I'll help out in Max's shop from time to time.

4. It will take time to make the shop look good.

**Note:** The letters s and h go together to stand for the sh sound in the word shop.

**C. Look down and across. Find the words in the box. Circle them.**

shop
take
records

| h | r | e | c | o | r | d | s |
|---|---|---|---|---|---|---|---|
| s | v | t | b | d | l | g | h |
| u | y | t | a | k | e | f | o |
| a | j | i | q | t | m | z | p |

**D. Write the word that best completes each sentence.**

record   take   shop

1. Max will keep a _____ of the store's sales.

2. People can't _____ for tapes in Max's Music Store.

3. I see that it will _____ a lot of work to save the store.

**E. Write your own sentence. Use one of the new words.**

_____

**Instructor's Notes:** Read each set of directions with students. Read each sight word aloud. Have students repeat. Read the sh note in the box. Ask students for other examples of words that begin with sh. Tell students that shop can be used as a noun or a verb. In D, point out another meaning for record: "facts that are written down."

## video • down • value

**A. Read the words above. Then read the sentence.**

Will this video go down in value?

**B. Underline the new words in sentences 1–4.**

1. Sales are down in Max's store.

2. I'll talk to him about the value of selling videos.

3. He can both rent and sell videos at the shop.

4. Max will see the value in this plan.

**C. Write the letters in the order that makes a word.**

lvuae _____value_____

wond _____

evodi _____

**D. Write the word that best completes each sentence.**

    value    videos    down

1. When we go _____ to the shop, Max and I find lots of people.

2. They can see our store has a lot of _____ for sale.

3. Max sees the _____ in selling tapes and videos.

**E. Write your own sentence. Use one of the new words.**

_____

**Instructor's Notes:** Read each set of directions with students. Encourage students to practice writing sentences from Review Words and Sight Words pages in a notebook or journal. Have students practice changing statements to questions.

7

Unit 1

# Phonics — Short e

**-ell**
sell
fell
tell
well
shell

**A. Read the words on the left. Write other -ell words.**

b + ell = __bell__

D + ell = _____

N + ell = _____

y + ell = _____

**B. Read the sentences. Circle the words with -ell. Write them.**

1. Max's music shop was not doing well. __well__

2. Can you see why the store fell on bad times? _____

3. What is Max going to sell in his store? _____

4. Tell some friends to stop by the store. _____

**C. Look across. Find the new words. Mark out letters that do not belong in each new word.**

1. ~~X~~ Y E L L ~~G~~ ~~H~~
2. P Z W E L L J
3. A M U B E L L
4. K F E L L S X

**D. Write your own sentence. Use an -ell word.**

_____

_____

**Instructor's Notes:** Show students the -ell word pattern in the known sight word *sell*. Then read each set of directions with students. For A, tell students that the words have the short e vowel sound. Review the *sh* sound in *shell*.

# Phonics — Long a

-ake
take
fake
make
sake
shake

**A. Read the words on the left. Write other -ake words.**

b + ake = _____

l + ake = _____

r + ake = _____

w + ake = _____

**B. Read the sentences. Circle the words with -ake. Write them.**

1. Max did take a good look at his shop. _____

2. He can make money selling videos. _____

3. Max had to wake up to what people are buying.

   _____

4. I am helping out for Max's sake. _____

**C. Circle the right word in each sentence.**

1. Max will find a plan to (make, bake) money.

2. He will do it for the (take, sake) of his family.

3. Max will (shake, take) a chance on renting videos.

4. Video stores can (rake, lake) in the money.

**D. Write your own sentence. Use an -ake word.**

_____

_____

**Instructor's Notes:** Show students the *-ake* word pattern in the known sight word *take*. Then read each set of directions with students. For A, tell students that the words have the long *a* vowel sound. Remind students that when words in the *cvc + e* pattern end in a silent *e*, the preceding vowel sound is usually long.

## Writing Skills — Compound Words

> Sometimes two words are joined together to make a new word with a different meaning. The new word is called a compound word.
>
> video + tape = videotape      home + sick = homesick

**A. Read the words. Write the new words.**

1. sail + boat = __sailboat__
2. some + times = _____
3. down + hill = _____
4. base + ball = _____
5. gold + fish = _____

**B. Draw lines to match the two words that make a compound word.**

1. home        stand
2. skate       one
3. pan         board
4. band        sick
5. some        cake

**C. Write the two words that make up each compound word.**

1. baseball    __base__         __ball__
2. workout     _____       _____
3. seasick     _____       _____
4. teacup      _____       _____

**Instructor's Notes:** Read the examples together and then the explanation in the box. Read each set of directions with students.

5. downhill  _____  _____

6. newspaper  _____  _____

**D. Read the compound words. Write the word that best fits in each sentence.**

**downhill   newspaper   workout   videotapes   sometimes**

Sales at the music store are going _____. Max will write an ad for the _____. Max loves the store, but _____ he feels like quitting. I tell Max to have _____ to rent. People who like to keep fit will use the _____ tapes. Max will have to take a chance to save the store.

**E. Read the sentences. Circle the compound words.**

Max set up some videotapes on a tabletop. He had music videos and workout tapes. He also had tapes for baseball fans. There is even a tape for people who have goldfish. I hope people will rent tapes from Max.

**F. Think about what Max could do. Write two sentences telling your ideas. Use a compound word in each sentence.**

1. _____

2. _____

**Instructor's Notes:** Read the directions with students. For F, brainstorm a list of compound words that students can choose from for their sentences.

### Back to the story...

**Remember**
What has happened in the story so far?

**Predict**
Look at the picture. What do you think will happen in the rest of the story?

# A Plan to Save the Store

Kent: Look at all the videos, tapes, and CDs you have! Max, how did you get the money for all of this?

Max: I came up with a sales plan and talked to some friends. It was a good plan, and they lent me the money. I had to take a chance, Kent.

Kent: It was time to take a chance. People like to buy tapes and CDs.

Max: I see that, Kent. And with all these tapes, videos, and CDs, how can you lose?

At the end of the day, Max sits down at his desk. He makes a record of the store's sales. This job takes time, but keeping good records is the key to running a shop that makes money. Max has to keep up with what people like.

Sales are bigger in Max's store. He sells a lot of tapes and CDs. People like pop, big band, rap, and country music. Videotape sales are bigger than music sales in Max's shop. Max keeps tapes for people of all ages. He has videos like "The Jetsons" for children and "Batman" for all the family. Max finds that a lot of people like workout videos. When people buy workout videos, they have fun and get fit.

Kent: Well, big brother, it looks like the plan to save Max's Music Store worked. Look at all the people, the videos, the CDs, and the tapes. How about that!

Max: I got lucky, Kent. But it wasn't all luck. It was a brother like you who helped me see the value of a good plan, and some friends with money helped me.

**Instructor's Notes:** Read the story pages with students or have them read silently.

Kent: I can see how you've worked. I'll bet you feel good.

Max: It feels good to pay back the friends who lent me money. I feel good that I didn't quit.

Kent: Do you still find time to work on the old guitars? A lot of people say you are good at fixing them.

Max: Yes, but doing a good job takes a lot of time. To keep up with my work on the guitars, I'll have to get someone to help out in the shop. Kent, how about working with me in the store?

Kent: Well, I didn't plan on this. But it will be fun to work in the store with you. How can we lose with a good plan, a lot of work, and good luck?

## Comprehension

**Think About It**
1. Why was Max's store losing money?
2. How did he change the store?
3. When did the store start to make money?
4. Sum up what happened in the story.

**Write About It**
What do you think is the key to success in running a business?

**Instructor's Notes:** Help students read and answer the questions. Write About It can be used as a writing or discussion assignment. Use the Unit 1 Review on page 15 to conclude the unit. Then assign *Reading for Today Workbook Three*, Unit 1.

**A. Complete each sentence. Use each word only once.**

tapes   sells   take   records   video   value   down

1. The store _____ guitars and _____ .

2. People like to buy music on _____ .

3. Sales are _____ in the store.

4. The _____ of the shop may go down.

**B. Write -ell or -ake to make new words. Write the word that fits best in each sentence.**

1. s + _____ = _____   I _____ records in my store.

2. w + _____ = _____   Records don't sell as _____ as they did.

3. t + _____ = _____   It will _____ a good plan to save the store.

4. m + _____ = _____   My brother will help me _____ a plan.

**C. Read each sentence. Find the compound word and write it.**

1. Sometimes my brother plays a guitar. _____

2. I am upset about the store. _____

3. Sales in my shop are going downhill. _____

4. Workout videos sell well. _____

5. People like to rent videotapes. _____

15

Unit 1

# Unit 2  Rearing Children

## Discussion

**Remember**

Look at the picture. What can a photo album tell about your past?

**Predict**

Look at the picture and the story title. What do you think the story is about?

# Looking Out for Me

I've had a lot of mothers and fathers. My brother Ed and I went from home to home. We had some good times and some bad times. Some of the people did love children and helped us. Some people didn't like us at all. At my age I can look at all this and laugh, but I feel I have lots of troubles to work out.

*The story continues.*

### A. Check the words you know.

- ☐ 1. age
- ☐ 2. brother
- ☐ 3. children
- ☐ 4. father
- ☐ 5. feel
- ☐ 6. find
- ☐ 7. from
- ☐ 8. laugh
- ☐ 9. lucky
- ☐ 10. mother
- ☐ 11. them
- ☐ 12. went

### B. Read and write the sentences. Circle the review words.

1. My brother and I went from home to home.

   _____

2. Some children end up in a bad home.

   _____

3. I feel like Nell and Bill are my mother and father.

   _____

4. They had time to talk and laugh with us.

   _____

5. At this age I can see that I was lucky to find them.

   _____

### C. Write a sentence. Use a review word.

_____

_____

**Instructor's Notes:** Read each set of directions with students. For A, have students read the words aloud and then check known words.

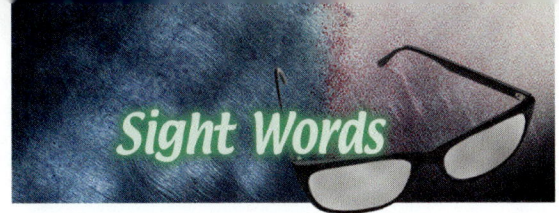 **Sight Words**

**parents • who • give**

**A. Read the words above. Then read the sentence.**

Some children have good **parents who give** them love.

**B. Underline the new words in sentences 1–4.**

1. Some people don't have children, but they can be parents.

2. They are people who have love to give.

3. They take in children who don't have parents.

4. They give the children food, love, and a good home.

**C. Look down and across. Find the words in the box. Circle them.**

give

parents

who

| b | f | u | g | w | h | o |
|---|---|---|---|---|---|---|
| k | e | w | i | m | j | q |
| h | o | c | v | r | l | d |
| p | a | r | e | n | t | s |

**D. Write the word that best completes each sentence.**

**give    who    parents**

1. The Lins are people _____ don't have children.

2. They feel that they can be good _____ .

3. The Lins can _____ a lot of love to children.

 **E. Write your own sentence. Use one of the new words.**

_____

**Instructor's Notes:** Read each set of directions with students. Read each sight word aloud. Have students repeat.

# Sight Words

own • fine • life

**A. Read the words above. Then read the sentence.**

My **own** parents didn't have a **fine life**.

**B. Underline the new words in sentences 1–4.**

1. My father was in fine health, but he got sick.

2. Mother had a lot of trouble in her life.

3. Her own parents didn't love her.

4. Mother's life wasn't good, but she didn't give up.

**C. Write the three new words into the puzzle.**

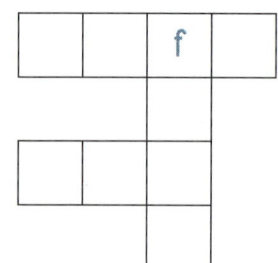

**D. Write the word that best completes each sentence.**

own    life    fine

1. Ed and I had a chance for a good _____ .

2. We had a _____ home with Bill and Nell Lin.

3. It was sad that our _____ parents didn't help us.

**E. Write your own sentence. Use one of the new words.**

_____

**Instructor's Notes:** Read each set of directions with students. Read each sight word aloud. Have students repeat.

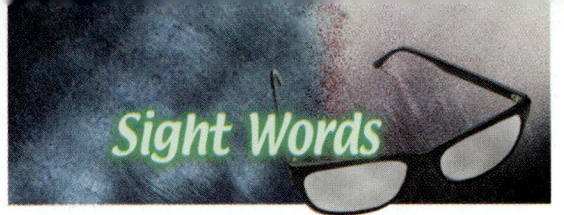

**Sight Words**  hug • social worker  when

**A. Read the words above. Then read the sentence.**

We got a **hug** from the **social worker when** we got to our home.

**B. Underline the new words in sentences 1–4.**

1. When my father got sick, he had to give up his job.

2. The social worker had to find us a home.

3. Dad gave Ed and me a big hug when we went.

4. The social worker helped us find Bill and Nell.

**Note:** The letters <u>w</u> and <u>h</u> go together to stand for the <u>wh</u> sound in the word <u>when</u>.

**C. Write the letters in the order that makes a word.**

guh _____

lciosa krowre _____  _____

henw _____

**D. Write the word that best completes each sentence.**

> hugs    when    social worker

1. Our _____ _____ helped us find a good family.

2. Kids get upset _____ they feel no one loves them.

3. A lot of _____ can make a kid feel good.

**E. Write your own sentence. Use one of the new words.**

_____

**Instructor's Notes:** Read each set of directions with students. Read each sight word aloud. Have students repeat. Read the *wh* note in the box. Ask for other words that begin with *wh*.

21

Unit 2

# Phonics: Short u

-ug
hug
bug
dug
rug

**A. Read the words on the left. Write other -ug words.**

j + ug = _____

l + ug = _____

m + ug = _____

t + ug = _____

**B. Read the sentences. Circle the words with -ug. Write them.**

1. We got a jug of water to take with us. _____

2. We have an old rug to sit down on. _____

3. I bet the bugs will bite us. _____

4. The car dug a hole in the wet sand. _____

**C. Look across. Find the new words. Mark out letters that do not belong in each new word.**

1. Q L U G K
2. T U G K X
3. V B C U G
4. G H U G H

**D. Write your own sentence. Use an -ug word.**

_____

_____

**Instructor's Notes:** Show students the -ug word pattern in the known sight word *hug*. Then read each set of directions with students. For A, tell students that a single vowel in a word ending in a consonant usually stands for the short vowel sound.

## Phonics: Long i

**-ine**
fine
line
nine
wine
shine

**A. Read the words on the left. Write other -ine words.**

d +ine = _____

m +ine = _____

p +ine = _____

v +ine = _____

wh +ine = _____

**B. Read the sentences. Circle the words with -ine. Write them.**

1. When I was nine, Nell let me get a dog. _____

2. We had a fine time playing games. _____

3. All dogs whine from time to time. _____

4. Owners have to learn to keep a dog in line. _____

**C. Circle the right word in each sentence.**

1. Don't (vine, shine) the light in my eyes.

2. A friend of (mine, pine) is working with children.

3. The family will (dine, line) at seven.

4. The old table is made of (shine, pine).

**D. Write your own sentence. Use an -ine word.**

_____

_____

**Instructor's Notes:** Show students the *-ine* word pattern in the known sight word *fine*. Then read each set of directions with students. For A, remind students that the *-ine* word family fits the *cvc + e* pattern. Vowels that follow this pattern are usually long.

## Writing Skills: Irregular Plurals

> Some words do not add **-s** or **-es** to mean more than one. These words have a different spelling for the plural.
>
> child    children      mouse    mice

**A. Read the words. Write the words that mean more than one.**

| One | More Than One | |
|---|---|---|
| woman | women | women |
| life | lives | _____ |
| leaf | leaves | _____ |
| foot | feet | _____ |
| man | men | _____ |
| person | people | _____ |

**B. Read each pair of sentences. Underline the words that are plurals.**

1. Ed is a good brother.
   Lots of men are good brothers.

2. Jean's father hurt his feet.
   Her father hurt one foot.

3. The social worker is a woman.
   Some women are nurses.

4. I plan to have a good life.
   My sisters had good lives.

**C. Read the sentences. Circle all the plural words.**

Ed and I have had trouble in our lives. We are lucky that social workers helped us. We met men and women who loved us and gave us good homes. Children without good parents can give up on life. With help from people who give them a chance, kids can do well.

**Instructor's Notes:** Read and discuss the examples with students. Read each set of directions. Explain that some words form plurals by changing letters in the words, not by adding *-s* or *-es* as most words do. For B and C, remind students to mark both regular and irregular plurals.

**D. Draw a line to match each word with its plural.**

1. mouse          people
2. person         men
3. child          leaves
4. woman          socks
5. sock           buses
6. leaf           mice
7. man            children
8. bus            women

**E. Write one of these words in each sentence.**

**children    feet    men    Women**

1. _____ are not the only ones who take care of kids.

2. When _____ are fathers, they need to help out.

3. Parents help their _____ .

4. Kids need help getting socks and shoes on their _____ .

**F. Write three sentences about family life. Use a plural word in each sentence.**

1. _____

2. _____

3. _____

**Instructor's Notes:** Read each set of directions with students. For F, discuss what students want to say about family life and help them write their sentences.

> **Back to the story...**
>
> **Remember**
> What has happened in the story so far?
>
> **Predict**
> Look at the picture. What job does the young woman have? How do you think her life will turn out?

# Looking Out for Me

When Dad got sick, the social worker had to take us. I went to the Light family, and Ed went to the Hanes. I didn't see Ed for some time, and I was sad about that. My brother is a good person. He is all the family I have.

But time is going on. I'm a woman of 18. When I got to be this age, I went out on my own. The social worker helped me get a job at the lake. I like the water, and I like to work with children. I'm doing a lot with my life.

For the time being, I have a home with a friend of mine. We get by, but I won't stop at this. With work and luck, I can have children of my own. I can make a good home for my family.

You can bet I'll be a good mother! I'll give my children all my love. I'll see that my kids eat well. I won't yell at them when they make mistakes. I'll see that my children have a father who is a fine man.

If my children have troubles, we will learn to talk it out. A family who can learn to talk about troubles will do fine.

When I was a child, I had a chance to learn the value of a good family. I met some fine men and women. When I have my own family, I'll be a good parent like Nell and Bill Lin. The Lins helped me see that having good parents gives a child a chance to do well in life.

Sometimes I feel sad like my mother did. When life gets me down, I find a friend to talk with. Sometimes a big hug is all it takes. I won't let my chances go by. My life is my own, and I'll make it a good one.

## Comprehension

**Think About It**

1. What kind of childhood did the girl and her brother have?
2. Who helped the children most? Why do you think so?
3. What did the girl learn from her experiences with the families she lived with?
4. Sum up what happened in the story.

**Write About It**

Do you think the young woman in this story is unusual? Explain why or why not.

**Instructor's Notes:** Help students read and answer the questions. Write About It can be used as a writing or discussion assignment. Use the Unit 2 Review on page 29 to conclude the unit. Then assign *Reading for Today Workbook Three*, Unit 2.

# Unit 2 Review

**A. Complete each sentence. Use each word only once.**

    hug   social worker   give   own   parents   life   when

1. Some children have _____ who _____ them love.

2. My _____ parents didn't have a fine _____.

3. The _____ _____ helped us find a home.

4. I'll _____ my children _____ I have my own.

**B. Write -ug or -ine to make new words. Write the word that fits best in each sentence.**

1. h + _____ = _____ I got a _____ from Bill.

2. r + _____ = _____ I got water on the _____.

3. f + _____ = _____ I had a _____ life with Nell.

4. n + _____ = _____ I was _____ when I got a dog.

**C. Write the word that fits best in each sentence.**

1. One _____ loved us.
    woman   women

2. All of her _____ played with us.
    child   children

3. _____ children liked us.
    This   These

4. All the _____ in the family helped us.
    man   men

# Unit 3  Promoting Health Care

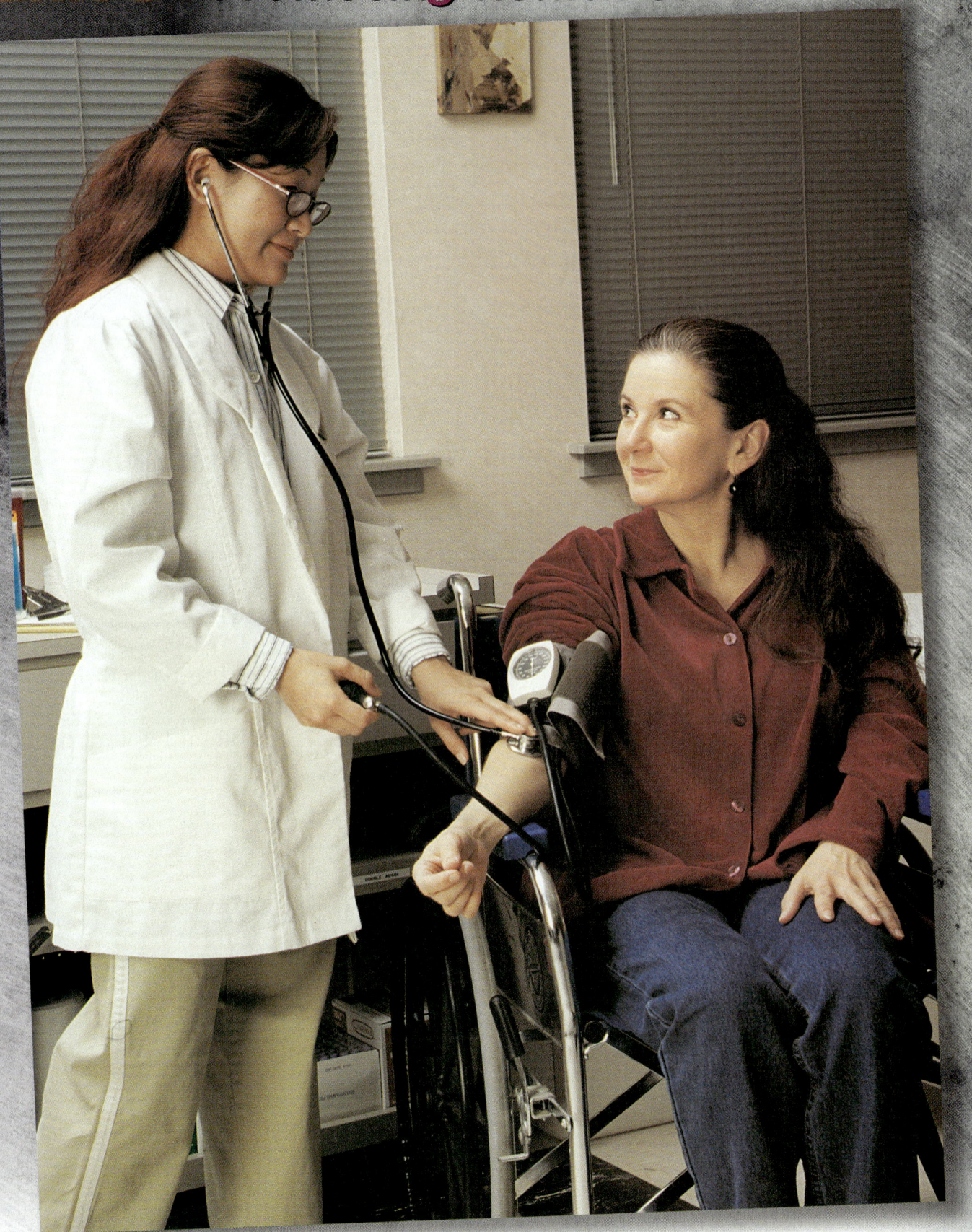

> **Discussion**
>
> **Remember**
> Look at the picture. Where does the story take place? Have you ever been to a place like this?
>
> **Predict**
> Look at the picture and the story title. What do you think this story is about?

# In Good Health

My job is helping people who are sick. I see people of all ages. When people are in bad health, I work to help make them well.

I work with nurses and with social workers. The nurses talk to parents about family health. The social workers talk to people who have troubles or feel sad when they walk in.

We can't win all the time, but we do our job.

*The story continues.*

**Instructor's Notes:** Read the discussion questions with students. Discuss the story title, the characters, and the situation in the picture. Have students read silently, or read the story with them. Have students underline words they don't recognize. Review the underlined words. Have students identify the speaker.

# Review Words

**A. Check the words you know.**

☐ 1. about   ☐ 2. but   ☐ 3. chance

☐ 4. fine   ☐ 5. glasses   ☐ 6. group

☐ 7. health   ☐ 8. nurse   ☐ 9. smoke

☐ 10. smoking   ☐ 11. social worker   ☐ 12. talk

**B. Read and write the sentences. Circle the review words.**

1. When a mother smokes, she takes a chance with her child's health.

   _____

2. Our social worker can get glasses for people who don't have money.

   _____

3. A nurse talks to groups about family health.

   _____

4. When I eat well, I feel fine.

   _____

5. I have to quit smoking, but I can't give it up.

   _____

**C. Write a sentence. Use a review word.**

_____

**Instructor's Notes:** Read each set of directions with students. For A, have students read the words aloud and then check known words.

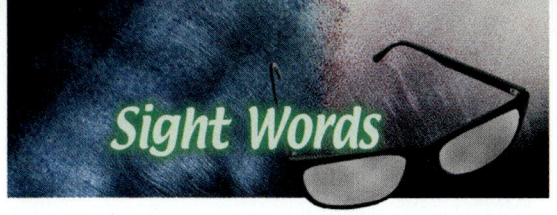

# Sight Words

clinic • hope • doctor

**A. Read the words above. Then read the sentence.**

People who go to a **clinic hope** the **doctor** can help them.

**B. Underline the new words in sentences 1–3.**

1. At a good clinic, all who walk in get help.

2. People hope the doctor can tell them what to do.

3. At the clinic, the doctor helps people get well.

**Note:** The letters c and l go together to stand for the cl sound in the word clinic.

**C. Write the three new words into the puzzle.**

**D. Write the word that best completes each sentence.**

**hopes    doctor    clinic**

1. Dan went to see the _____ about his smoking.

2. The doctor sent Dan to a group at the _____ .

3. Dan _____ to quit smoking with the group's help.

**E. Write your own sentence. Use one of the new words.**

_____

**Instructor's Notes:** Read each set of directions with students. Read each sight word aloud. Have students repeat. Read the cl note in the box. Ask students for other words that begin with cl.

33

Unit 3

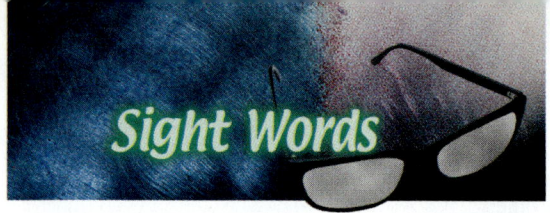

# Sight Words

what • problem • said

**A.** Read the words above. Then read the sentences.

**What problem** do you have?
The nurse **said** she can help.

**B.** Underline the new words in sentences 1–4.

1. The woman said her hand wasn't mending.

2. What can she do about this problem?

3. The nurse can tell the woman what to do.

4. The nurse can help her work on the problem.

**Note:** The letters p and r go together to stand for the pr sound in the word problem.

**C.** Write the letters in the order that makes a word.

adis  _____

brelmop  _____

tahw  _____

**D.** Write the word that best completes each sentence.

problems    said    what

1. Doctors at the clinic see lots of _____ .

2. The doctors tell people _____ to do to get well.

3. The nurse _____ the clinic gives people hope.

**E.** Write your own sentence. Use one of the new words.

_____

**Instructor's Notes:** Read each set of directions with students. Read each sight word aloud. Have students repeat. Read the *pr* note in the box. Ask students for other words that begin with *pr*.

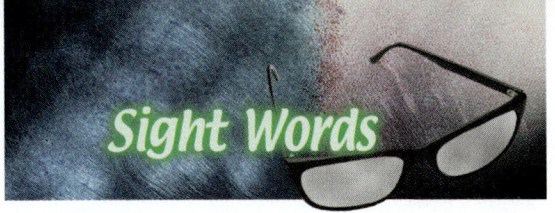

# Sight Words

### want • more • hip

**A. Read the words above. Then read the sentence.**

I **want more** help for my bad **hip**.

**B. Underline the new words in sentences 1–4.**

1. Nan wants to see the doctor about her hip.

2. Standing and sitting makes her hip feel bad.

3. The doctor wants Nan to walk more.

4. He said more walking is good for her hip.

**C. Look down and across. Find the words in the box. Circle them.**

want
more
hip

| r | m | c | g | e | v | w |
|---|---|---|---|---|---|---|
| z | o | w | a | n | t | b |
| s | r | d | h | i | p | l |
| k | e | f | y | u | w | q |
| c | h | j | k | e | b | x |

**D. Write the word that best completes each sentence.**

    want    more    hip

1. I have trouble with my _____ .

2. I _____ to do what the doctor said.

3. I don't want _____ health problems.

**E. Write your own sentence. Use one of the new words.**

_____

**Instructor's Notes:** Read each set of directions with students. Read each sight word aloud. Have students repeat.

# Phonics   Short i

**A. Read the words on the left. Write other -ip words.**

-ip
hip
lip
sip
tip
clip
ship

d + ip = _____

n + ip = _____

r + ip = _____

z + ip = _____

**B. Read the sentences. Circle the words with -ip. Write them.**

1. The nurse has lots of health tips. _____

2. When the child fell down, he cut his lip. _____

3. A sip of cold water will help. _____

**C. Look across. Find the new words. Mark out letters that do not belong in each new word.**

1. T N I P V
2. E C L I P
3. T M R I P
4. S H I P Z
5. G A Z I P

**D. Write your own sentence. Use an -ip word.**

_____

_____

**Instructor's Notes:** Show students the *-ip* word pattern in the known sight word *hip*. Then read each set of directions with students. For A, tell students that the *i* in *hip* stands for the short vowel sound. Review the *cl* sound in *clip*.

# Phonics: Long o

**-ope**
**hope**
**cope**
**rope**

**A. Read the words on the left. Write other -ope words.**

l + ope = _____

m + ope = _____

p + ope = _____

**B. Read the sentences. Circle the words with -ope. Write them.**

1. Jan feels that she has no hope of getting well.

   _____

2. She sits at home and mopes about her problems.

   _____

3. Jan can't cope with bad health. _____

4. I hope that Jan will get well. _____

**C. Circle the right word in each sentence.**

1. We all have to (cope, lope) with health problems from time to time.

2. It's my job to make the beds, but I can (mope, rope) Ned into helping me.

**D. Write your own sentence. Use an -ope word.**

_____

_____

**Instructor's Notes:** Show students the -ope word pattern in the known sight word *hope*. Then read each set of directions with students. For A, remind students that the -ope word family fits the *cvc + e* pattern. Vowels in this pattern are usually long.

## Writing Skills

# Adding -er to Naming Words

**You can add -er to some words to make a new word. A worker is someone who works. A smoker is someone who smokes. If a word ends in "e" like smoke, drop the e before adding -er.**

work + er = worker     smoke + er = smoker

**A. Add -er. Write the new words.**

1. buy + er = _____
2. help + er = _____
3. read + er = _____
4. smoke + er = _____
5. talk + er = _____
6. play + er = _____

**B. Read the sentences. Underline the words that end in -er.**

Ned Cutman was a smoker. When he quit, he wanted to be a helper at the health clinic. Sometimes he helps with the children. Ned is a good reader. He is a big talker. He is the one worker who makes the children laugh. He is a big seller of good health.

**C. Draw a line to match each -er word with the word it came from.**

1. talker      own
2. buyer      smoke
3. smoker     make
4. owner      talk
5. maker      buy

**Instructor's Notes:** Read each set of directions with students. Discuss the examples and point out the slash through the *e* in *smoke*. Explain that the *e* is dropped when *-er* is added. Or, in practical terms, as many students will observe, just add *-r* to a word that already ends in *e*. Explain that adding *-er* to verbs changes them to nouns.

**D. Make new words by adding -er. Write the words.**

1. tell   _____

2. walk   _____

3. fake   _____

4. sell   _____

5. shake   _____

6. pay   _____

**E. Write the word that fits best in each sentence.**

**helper    talker    reader    smoker    worker**

1. Ned Cutman is a man who was a _____ .

2. He wanted to be a _____ at the clinic.

3. Ned is a good _____ .

4. Ned is a big _____ .

5. The clinic is lucky to have a _____ like Ned.

**F. Think about workers or helpers you know. Write three sentences. Use a word with an -er ending in each sentence.**

1. _____

2. _____

3. _____

**Instructor's Notes:** Read each set of directions with students. For F, brainstorm a list of words ending with -er that students might use in their sentences.

### Back to the story...

**Remember**
What has happened in the story so far?

**Predict**
Look at the picture. What do you think will happen in the rest of the story?

## Daily Log

| | |
|---|---|
| | Pat R., age 8
Problem: A dog nipped Pat's hand. I talked to Pat, to her father, and to the dog's owner. He said that the dog is in good health. Pat will be fine. Her hand looks OK. |
| 8:30 A.M. | Jake B., age 32
Problem: Jake can't cope with his family's problems. I sent him to the clinic social worker. He tells me that Jake and his family want to go into a group for some help. |
| 9:00 A.M. | Jed P., age 19
Problem: Jed has trouble when he eats the wrong foods. I want him to stop eating dips, nuts, and cake. Jed said he will do what I want. I'll send him to a doctor who can help us find out more about the foods that are bad for him. |

# Daily Log

| 9:15 A.M. | Van A, age 63 |
|---|---|
| | Problem: Van smokes, but at his age, he feels that he can't stop. In time he will have more and more problems. I want him to go to the clinic's stop smoking group. Without this group, I don't have a lot of hope for the smoker. |
| 9:45 A.M. | Lin H., age 52 |
| | Problem: Lin feels down and out. Her health is good, but she sits at home all the time. She mopes about her life. She has to get out and see people. This will give her a chance to make friends. I'll talk to the social worker about this. |
| 10:30 A.M. | Dot S., age 2 |
| | Problem: Dot has a big red cut on her lip. It looks like someone hit her. She won't eat. I went to see Dot's parents, but they won't talk about it. Her home life isn't good. The social worker said I have to make a record of these problems. |

**Instructor's Notes:** Read the story pages with students or have them read silently.

## Daily Log

**11:00 A.M.** — Kip R., age 73
Problem: A man will be in with his father. The father fell down at the store and landed on his hip. I'll see him, but I have some more people to see by sundown.

**1:00 P.M.** — A social worker for the clinic wants me to talk to a group of children about the food they eat. They want me to tell them about good health.

**4:00 P.M.** — I've got some records to read. I hope I can get to this. I don't like to take work home.

**7:00 P.M.** — It's good that we love what we do at the clinic. Our work has no end to it. In time, we'll win the love of the people who use our clinic.

## Comprehension

### Think About It

1. What are the doctor's main responsibilities?
2. How does the doctor keep track of daily problems?
3. Do you think the doctor has a good method of keeping patient records? Why or why not?
4. Sum up what happened in the story.

### Write About It

How do you think the doctor feels about her job?

**Instructor's Notes:** Help students read and answer the questions. Write About It can be used as a writing or discussion assignment. Use the Unit 3 Review on page 43 to conclude the unit. Then assign *Reading for Today Workbook Three*, Unit 3.

# Unit 3 Review

**A. Complete each sentence. Use each word only once.**

clinic    said    doctor    what    hope    hip

1. The _____ at the _____ helps people.

2. The doctor _____ she can help me with my problem.

3. I _____ I can get help at the clinic.

4. I want my _____ to mend.

**B. Write -ip or -ope to make new words. Write the word that fits best in each sentence.**

1. h + _____ = _____ The man fell on his _____ .

2. t + _____ = _____ The nurse gives me a _____ .

3. h + _____ = _____ Jan can't give up _____ of getting well.

4. c + _____ = _____ She will _____ with the problem.

**C. Write the words that end in -er.**

1. Ned wanted to be a helper at the clinic. _____

2. He helped a baseball player with a cut lip. _____

3. Ned is a good worker at the clinic. _____

4. He helped a smoker to stop smoking. _____

5. The children said Ned is a good reader. _____

# Unit 4  Handling Social Relationships

## Discussion

**Remember**

Look at the picture. What do you think is happening? Have you worked on a team with other people?

**Predict**

Read the title of the story. How many men are working in the picture? What do you think this story is about?

# A Team at Work

Ray and I work at Big Value. We get to the store at 7:00 and we get out at 3:00. The work is a lot for two men. So we asked the boss, Jan, to get a third man to help us. Jan said OK.

But our helper, Jake, was no help at all! From the very first, he was a problem. He was late to work. When he got in, he sat and smoked. He did not lend a hand. He looked upset and mad a lot of the time.

It wasn't working out at all. Ray and I had to tell Jan about it.

*The story continues.*

# Review Words

**A. Check the words you know.**

☐ 1. boss ☐ 2. see ☐ 3. hope

☐ 4. helper ☐ 5. trouble ☐ 6. store

☐ 7. problem ☐ 8. play ☐ 9. hand

☐ 10. asked ☐ 11. lend ☐ 12. work

**B. Read and write the sentences. Circle the review words.**

1. The boss likes our work.

   _____

2. We hope Jake will be a helper.

   _____

3. Jake doesn't lend a hand at the store.

   _____

4. Will Jan see the trouble we have?

   _____

5. Jan asked about the problem.

   _____

**C. Write a sentence. Use a review word.**

_____

**Instructor's Notes:** Read each set of directions with students. For A, have students read the words aloud and then check known words.

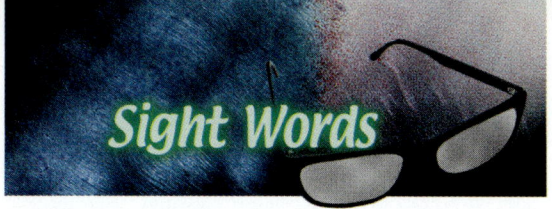

**need • team • load**

**A. Read the words above. Then read the sentence.**

We **need** to work like a **team**, but Jake will not help us **load**.

**B. Underline the new words in sentences 1–4.**

1. Ray and I are a team.

2. We need a third man.

3. Jan sees what we need.

4. Can Jake load from 7:00 to 3:00?

**C. Write the letters in the order that makes a new word.**

amte      _____

ndee      _____

daol      _____

**D. Write the word that best completes each sentence.**

**need    team    load**

1. We plan to _____ a lot of boxes.

2. We _____ Jake's help.

3. Jake is not a _____ worker.

**E. Write your own sentence. Use one of the new words.**

_____

**Instructor's Notes:** Read each set of directions with students. Read each sight word aloud and have students repeat it.

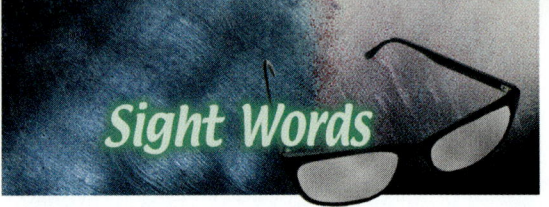

## Sight Words

day • does • uniform

**A. Read the words above. Then read the sentence.**

On the first **day**, Jake **does** not have his **uniform**.

**B. Underline the new words in sentences 1–4.**

1. The uniform has a name on it.

2. Jake feels the uniform does not fit him.

3. The day does not go well.

4. A day like this upsets Ray and me.

**C. Look down and across. Find the new words in the box. Circle them.**

day
does
uniform

| u | n | i | f | o | r | m |
|---|---|---|---|---|---|---|
| d | a | y | l | m | p | l |
| o | r | s | l | t | x | r |
| e | n | f | b | g | u | v |
| s | h | j | d | c | r | x |

**D. Write the word that best completes each sentence.**

**does   day   uniform**

1. Big Value workers have a _____ .

2. Jake _____ not like it.

3. Jake has a problem on the first _____ .

**E. Write your own sentence. Use one of the new words.**

_____

**Instructor's Notes:** Read each set of directions with students. Read each sight word aloud and have students repeat it.

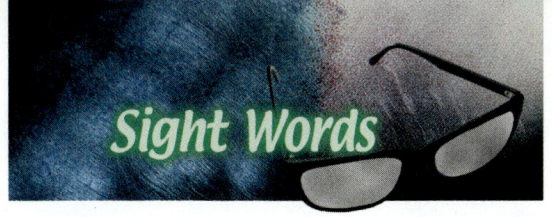

# Sight Words

because • cover • there

**A. Read the words above. Then read the sentence.**

We need Jake **because there** are a lot of boxes to **cover**.

**B. Underline the new words in sentences 1–3.**

1. We have to cover the boxes.

2. We do it because that's our job.

3. Are there more boxes in the store?

**Note:** The letters <u>t</u> and <u>h</u> go together to stand for the <u>th</u> sound in the words <u>there</u>, <u>that</u>, <u>them</u>, <u>they</u>, <u>the</u>, <u>this</u>, and <u>then</u>.

**C. Write the new words into the puzzle.**

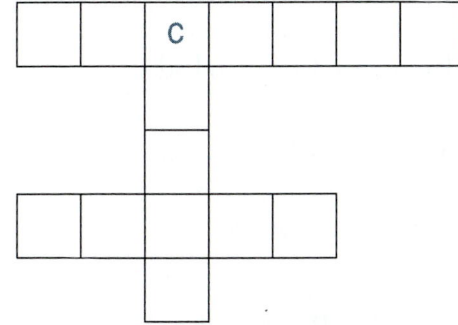

**D. Write the word that best completes each sentence.**

because    there    cover

1. We get mad _____ Jake doesn't help.

2. He sits _____ and looks at us.

3. We can't _____ up our feelings.

**E. Write your own sentence. Use one of the new words.**

_____

**Instructor's Notes:** Read each set of directions with students. Read each sight word aloud and have students repeat it.

## Phonics: Long a

A. Read the words on the left. Write other -ay words.

-ay
day
may
pay
way
clay
play

h + ay = _____

J + ay = _____

l + ay = _____

r + ay = _____

s + ay = _____

B. Read the sentences. Circle the words with -ay. Write them.

1. Jake may not fit our team. _____

2. Ray and I don't like the way he works! _____

3. One day, we will say this to Jan. _____

4. She will not pay Jake for bad work. _____

C. Look across. Find the new words. Mark out letters that do not belong in each new word.

1. Q H A Y X E
2. R T P A Y U
3. A C Z S A Y
4. J A Y L I W
5. T C L A Y F

D. Write your own sentence. Use an -ay word.

_____

**Instructor's Notes:** Show students the -ay word pattern in the known sight word *day*. Then read each set of directions with students. For A, tell students that -ay stands for the long *a* vowel sound.

50

Unit 4

# Phonics: Long e

-eed
need
deed
feed
heed

**A. Read the words on the left. Write other -eed words.**

r + eed = _____

s + eed = _____

w + eed = _____

**B. Read the sentences. Circle the words with -eed. Write them.**

1. Jake does not help Ray load seed at the store. _____

2. Ray and I need to talk to Jan about this. _____

3. That will be a good deed for our boss. _____

4. Jan needs to weed out problems at work. _____

**C. Circle the right word in each sentence.**

1. Ray and I cut the (seeds, weeds) on the Big Value lot.

2. We (deed, need) uniforms on our job.

3. It takes a lot of our pay to (feed, reed) the family.

4. (Deed, Heed) my words: It pays to work as a team!

**D. Write your own sentences. Use an -eed word in each one.**

1. _____

2. _____

3. _____

**Instructor's Notes:** Show students the -eed word pattern in *need*. Then read the directions with students. For A, tell students that -ee stands for the long e vowel sound. Explain that when two vowels are side by side, the first vowel is usually long and the second is silent. Examples include the -ee in need and the -ea in *team*.

# Using Commas

> Use a comma to separate words in a series.
> I have a family, a job, and some money.
> Jan, Ray, and I talked.
> Use a comma after an introductory word.
> Jan, we need to talk to you.
> Well, Jake is late to work.
> Use a comma to separate parts of a date.
> I got this job on May 8, 1999.

**A. Read the sentences. Then write them.**

1. We work, eat, and laugh.

   _____

2. Ray, help me with this box.

   _____

3. Jake came to work on June 5, 2000.

   _____

4. We lug boxes, desks, and beds.

   _____

5. No, Jake will not help.

   _____

6. Jan, what can we do?

   _____

**Instructor's Notes:** Read the explanation in the box and discuss the examples. Point out and demonstrate by reading aloud that a comma shows a place to pause slightly when you're reading.

**B. Add a comma in each space. Then write the sentence.**

1. I work __ do my job __ and get my pay.

   _____

2. Jake __ what is your problem?

   _____

3. It was June 6 __ 2000.

   _____

4. Jake sat __ looked __ and didn't help.

   _____

**C. Write each sentence. Add commas where they belong.**

1. I work help and laugh with Ray.

2. It is May 8 2000.

3. Ray are you mad at Jake?

**D. Write three sentences. Use commas correctly.**

1. A sentence that separates words in a series

   _____

2. A sentence that starts with an introductory word

   _____

3. A sentence that has a date

   _____

*Back to the story...*

**Remember**
What has happened in the story so far?

**Predict**
Look at the picture. What do you think will happen in the rest of the story?

# A Team at Work

Jan: Yes, I see you have a big problem with Jake. Let me give you some tips about how to get him on the team. One, don't get mad and yell at Jake. Yelling makes the problem bigger.

Sam: So, don't we tell Jake what we feel about him?

Ray: What do we do?

Jan: Tip two, talk about the job, not about people. Tell Jake about a day here at Big Value. What is the first job of the day? What is the last one? You know this job well because you've been at it for some time. But it's all a first for Jake!

Sam: Then what?

**Instructor's Notes:** Read the questions with students. Help them review and predict. Point out that the names on the left show who is speaking in the story. Read the story aloud to students, or have them read silently, or have them read aloud, taking on the various roles.

Jan: Third, find out what Jake's own problems are with the job. Let him talk and tell you.

Ray: What good will that do?

Jan: Jake will learn a lot about the job when you talk. Now you will learn about Jake when he talks!

Sam: How will that help?

Jan: It's a way to see what help Jake needs. He can't help you if you don't help him.

Ray: Is there more we need to do?

Jan: Yes, there's a fourth tip. It's for the three of you to make a work plan for the day. Do it when you get to work, and do it like a team.

Ray and I used the first two tips. First, we talked to Jake about the problems we run into at work. Jake didn't look at us when we talked. That made me mad, but I didn't yell. Jan had said not to. But it looked like Jake had tuned us out. What good was it to go on to tips three and four? Then Jake looked up.

Jake: This talk is what I needed. At first it seemed like you two didn't need me on your team. But you've helped me see what I can do to help. Can we talk about a work plan for the three of us?

Ray and I had to laugh! Jake had covered tips three and four for us! So that's the way it went. The three of us made a work plan. Today we are a fine team. It's all because of four tips for talking about a problem.

## Comprehension

**Think About It**

1. Why were Ray and Sam angry at Jake?
2. What four tips did Jan give Ray and Sam?
3. Why did Jake just sit around on his first days at work?
4. Sum up what happened in the story.

**Write About It**

What kind of help do you need on your first day at a new job?

**Instructor's Notes:** Help students read and answer the questions. Use Write About It as a writing or discussion assignment. Use the Unit 4 Review on the next page to conclude the unit. Then assign *Reading for Today Workbook Three*, Unit 4.

**A. Complete each sentence. Use each word only once.**

team    load    day    uniform    because    there

1. The day went well _____ we worked like a team.

2. He does not like his red _____ .

3. We need to _____ the boxes into the van.

4. Is _____ a cover for this box of records?

**B. Write -ay or -eed to make new words. Write the word that fits best in each sentence.**

1. n + _____ = _____    We _____ a helper.

2. w + _____ = _____    The boxes are in the _____ .

3. pl + _____ = _____    There's no time to _____ .

4. h + _____ = _____    We _____ Jan's words.

**C. Write the sentences. Add commas to make them correct.**

1. Jake can you help?

_____

2. It is June 8 2000.

_____

3. Yes he's here.

_____

4. Jake Ray and Sam are a team.

_____

# Unit 5  Learning About Training Programs

## Discussion

**Remember**

Look at the picture. What experiences have you had training or teaching an animal?

**Predict**

Look at the picture and the story title. What do you think this story is about?

# Helping Dogs to Help People

When I got in trouble with the cops, I had the feeling that my life was at an end. Today I see that life wasn't ending for me. I got into a group that works with dogs. We send the dogs out to people who need them.

Today I work with Sundown, a big, fine dog. I feed him and see that he has all the water he needs. When he does well, he gets a big hug from me.

The key to working with dogs is love. It's good to have this job because it gives me hope for my own life.

*The story continues.*

**Instructor's Notes:** Read the discussion questions with students. Discuss the story title, the characters, and the situation in the picture. Have students read silently or read together. Have students underline words they don't recognize. Review the underlined words. Have students identify the speaker.

# Review Words

**A. Check the words you know.**

☐ 1. be  ☐ 2. did  ☐ 3. do

☐ 4. does  ☐ 5. dog  ☐ 6. eat

☐ 7. eyes  ☐ 8. fed  ☐ 9. his

☐ 10. mistake  ☐ 11. my  ☐ 12. send

**B. Read and write the sentences. Circle the review words.**

1. My dog wants to do well, but sometimes he makes mistakes.

   _____

2. His eyes shine with pride when he does well.

   _____

3. Sundown likes to eat, and he will be fed two times a day.

   _____

4. Did Sundown eat all his food?

   _____

5. I send my dog out to play when his work ends.

   _____

**C. Write a sentence. Use a review word.**

_____

_____

**Instructor's Notes:** Read each set of directions with students. For A, have students read the words aloud and then check known words.

# Sight Words

prison • learn • teach

**A. Read the words above. Then read the sentence.**

In **prison** we **learn** to **teach** dogs.

**B. Underline the words in sentences 1–4.**

1. Not all prisons give people a chance like this.

2. The dogs we teach will help people someday.

3. The dogs learn to work with people who need them.

4. I hope I can use this prison job when I get out.

**C. Write the three new words into the puzzle.**

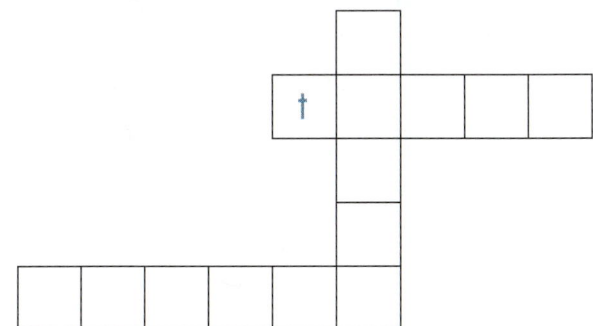

**D. Write the word that best completes each sentence.**

**learning    prison    teach**

1. Prison can _____ me to cope with life.

2. I'm _____ to use my time well.

3. I can't say that _____ is a lot of fun.

**E. Write your own sentence. Use one of the new words.**

_____

**Instructor's Notes:** Read each set of directions with students. Read each sight word aloud. Have students repeat.

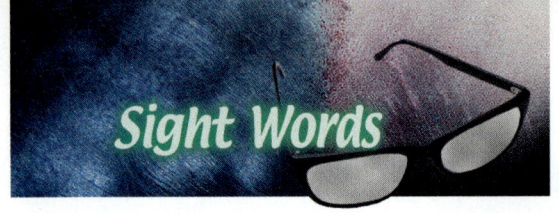

## Sight Words

**disabled** • **different** • **things**

**A. Read the words above. Then read the sentence.**

A **disabled** person can use a dog for **different things**.

**B. Underline the new words in sentences 1–4.**

1. We teach our dogs to do different things.

2. These dogs are helpers for disabled people.

3. People have different needs for our dogs.

4. Dogs help disabled people to get out.

**Note:** The letters <u>t</u> and <u>h</u> go together to stand for the <u>th</u> sound in <u>there</u>. But <u>th</u> can also stand for the whispered <u>th</u> sound in <u>thing</u> and <u>thin</u>.

**C. Write the letters in the order that makes a word.**

leddabis    _____

gtnihs      _____

fentfirde   _____

**D. Write the word that best completes each sentence.**

**disabled    different    things**

1. I am learning _____ ways to do _____ with my dog's help.

2. My dog has helped me see that being _____ is OK.

**E. Write your own sentence. Use one of the new words.**

_____

**Instructor's Notes:** Read each set of directions with students. Read each sight word aloud. Have students repeat. Read the *th* note in the box. Ask for other words that begin with *th*.

Unit 5

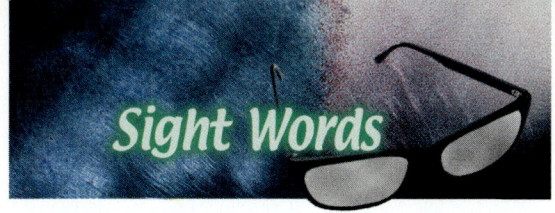

# Sight Words

June • come • right

**A. Read the words above. Then read the sentence.**

June said that the dog will come right to her.

**B. Underline the new words in sentences 1–4.**

1. June had to learn to work with her dog.

2. She learned the right way to tell the dog what to do.

3. The dog comes when June calls it.

4. June has the right dog for her needs.

**C. Look down and across. Find the words in the box. Circle them.**

come
June
right

| s | w | d | a | l | c | n |
|---|---|---|---|---|---|---|
| f | l | p | c | k | o | y |
| r | i | g | h | t | m | b |
| a | k | j | u | n | e | x |
| z | q | b | f | p | d | v |

**D. Write the word that best completes each sentence.**

June    right    come

1. Working with dogs is _____ for me.

2. It makes me feel good to help _____ .

3. The time will _____ when June will go home.

**E. Write your own sentence. Use one of the new words.**

_____

**Instructor's Notes:** Read each set of directions with students. Read each sight word aloud. Have students repeat.

# Phonics — Long i

-ight
right
fight
night
sight

**A. Read the words on the left. Write other -ight words.**

l + ight = _____

m + ight = _____

t + ight = _____

**B. Read the sentences. Circle the words with -ight. Write them.**

1. Our dogs help people with bad sight. _____

2. They are on the job day and night. _____

3. Disabled people need to find a dog that is right for them.

_____

**C. Look across. Find the new words. Mark out letters that do not belong in each new word.**

1. G F I G H T L
2. B C M I G H T
3. L I G H T J Z
4. E T I G H T A
5. D P N I G H T

**D. Write your own sentence. Use an -ight word.**

_____

_____

**Instructor's Notes:** Show students the -ight word pattern in the known sight word *right*. Then read each set of directions with students. For A, tell students that -igh often spells the long *i* vowel sound and that the letters *g* and *h* are silent.

# Phonics    Long u

**-une and -ute**
June
dune
tune
prune

**A. Read the words on the left. Write -ute words below.**

c + ute = _____

l + ute = _____

m + ute = _____

**B. Read the sentences. Circle the words with -une and -ute. Write them.**

1. Some disabled people can't talk. They are mute.

   _____

2. June has trouble getting about in the city because she can't see.

   _____

3. Her dog may be cute, but it isn't a pet. _____

**C. Circle the right word in each sentence.**

1. I want to learn that (tune, dune) on the radio.

2. The children played in the sand (dunes, prunes).

3. I learned to talk with my hands because I am (lute, mute).

4. My dog can do (cute, mute) things.

**D. Write your own sentence. Use a -une or -ute word.**

_____

_____

**Instructor's Notes:** Show students the -une word pattern in the known sight word *June*. Introduce the -ute word pattern. Then read each set of directions with students. For A, remind students that the -une and -ute word families fit the *cvc + e* pattern. Vowels that follow this pattern are usually long.

## Writing Skills: Irregular Verbs

> We add -ed to some words to show the past:
> work    work__ed__
> Other words change the spelling to show the past:
> grow    <u>grew</u>

**A. Write the words that show past time.**

| Present | Past | | Present | Past | |
|---------|------|--|---------|------|--|
| come | came | _____ | go | went | _____ |
| say | said | _____ | take | took | _____ |
| know | knew | _____ | give | gave | _____ |
| are | were | _____ | feed | fed | _____ |

**B. Practice reading the sentences. Circle the words that show past time.**

I came to this prison to do time. Some of the prisoners were working with dogs. One day I went to see them. They gave me a dog to work with. Working with Sundown took a lot of time, but helping out gave me a good feeling.

**C. Write the word that fits best in each sentence.**

grew    said    fed    knew

1. I _____ Sundown.

2. He _____ fast.

3. Sundown _____ his name.

4. I _____ it a lot when I worked with him.

**Instructor's Notes:** Read each set of directions with students. Discuss the examples. Explain that some verbs form the past tense by changing letters in the word, not by adding -ed. These verbs are called irregular verbs because they don't follow a regular pattern.

**D. Circle the verb in each sentence that shows past time. Write it.**

1. The dogs (are, **were**) not a problem. _____

2. We (take, **took**) them for walks. _____

3. The dogs (go, **went**) to disabled people. _____

4. Someone (come, **came**) to get Sundown. _____

5. I (say, **said**) he was a fine dog. _____

6. I (give, **gave**) Sundown a big hug. _____

**E. What time does the underlined verb in each sentence show? Circle present or past.**

1. I know Sundown is fine.          present    past

2. Dogs came here to learn.         present    past

3. We fed them at seven.            present    past

4. They go to good homes.           present    past

**F. Write three sentences about people and their dogs. Use an irregular past time verb in each sentence.**

1. _____

2. _____

3. _____

**Instructor's Notes:** Read each set of directions with students. For F, help students write their sentences.

> **Back to the story...**
>
> **Remember**
> What has happened in the story so far?
>
> **Predict**
> Look at the picture. What do you think will happen in the rest of the story?

# Helping Dogs to Help People

To June,

I hope you and Sundown are doing fine. He is a good dog and learned all the right things to help you. Sometimes I'm sad because he had to go. But Sundown isn't a pet—he's a working dog with a job to do.

These days I'm working with a different dog. Zip is a cute dog who likes to eat. He has a lot to learn, but I've got lots of time to teach him.

This job is helping me see that I've got something to give. Disabled people who want to use a dog might need my help. Teaching dogs to help people is a good thing for a woman in prison to learn.

Can you and Sundown come to see me? I send both of you my love.

To Fay,

Sundown and I are doing fine. We're learning different ways of getting about in the city. He walks me to the clinic and to see friends. My boss said I can take Sundown on the job. You were right. With Sundown's help, I can be on my own.

Sundown might not get homesick for the prison, but he does get homesick for you. You were his teacher. You fed him and gave him a lot of love.

When I came to the prison, I was about to give up. Today things are different. It took time, but I learned to do a lot of things without my sight. People who become disabled don't need to feel that life has ended.

To June,

Today I learned that I might get out of prison in May! What will I do? Maybe I can get a job helping disabled people. The social worker said she will help me find a job.

In the old days, I made a lot of mistakes. I ended up in prison. But when I get out, I will have a different life.

When I came to prison, it took some time to see that there was hope for my life. But today I feel I can make it on my own without getting in more trouble.

Good luck to you and Sundown.

## Comprehension

**Think About It**

1. What skill did Fay learn while she was in prison?
2. How do you think Fay feels about the dogs she trains?
3. When did June find her life getting better?
4. Sum up what happened in the story.

**Write About It**

What kind of work makes you feel most useful? Why?

**Instructor's Notes:** Help students read and answer the questions. Write About It can be used as a writing or discussion assignment. Use the Unit 5 Review on page 71 to conclude the unit. Then assign *Reading for Today Workbook Three*, Unit 5.

# Unit 5 Review

**A. Complete each sentence. Use each word only once.**

      **different    learn    disabled    come    prison**

1. In prison we _____ to teach dogs.

2. I teach the dogs to _____ to me.

3. The dogs help _____ people get about in the city.

4. People have _____ needs for our dogs.

**B. Write -ight or -une to make new words. Write the word that fits best in each sentence.**

1. m + _____ = _____   A disabled person _____ need a dog.

2. s + _____ = _____   June has learned to do things without her _____ .

3. f + _____ = _____   Dogs have to learn not to _____ .

4. J + _____ = _____   _____ uses a dog to help her be on her own.

**C. Draw lines to match the present tense of the word with the past tense.**

1. come         did

2. do            were

3. is             went

4. are          came

5. go           was

# Unit 6   Coping with Job Dissatisfaction

## Discussion

**Remember**

Look at the picture. What do you think is happening? What do you know about the day-to-day lives of truckers?

**Predict**

Look at the picture and the story title. What do you think this story is about?

# A Life on the Go

I'm on the go all the time. Sometimes I'm in the country, and sometimes I'm in a city. I'm on my own a lot of the time.

I want to have more time with my family—more time with Hope and my children, Mike and Pam. There are lots of holidays when I can't be at home with them.

I bet that a lot of people feel the way I do. But a job is a job, and this is the work I do. Being on the go all the time is my way of life.

*The story continues.*

# Review Words

**A. Check the words you know.**

☐ 1. ads  ☐ 2. bet  ☐ 3. bigger

☐ 4. fit  ☐ 5. hand  ☐ 6. holiday

☐ 7. no  ☐ 8. on  ☐ 9. read

☐ 10. son  ☐ 11. upset  ☐ 12. will

**B. Read and write the sentences. Circle the review words.**

1. I bet I won't make it home on the holidays.

   _____

2. My son will be upset about that.

   _____

3. I bet a job with a bigger store will fit my needs.

   _____

4. I read the ads, but there are no jobs for someone like me.

   _____

5. Maybe my friend Bill will give me a hand.

   _____

**C. Write a sentence. Use a review word.**

_____

**Instructor's Notes:** Read each set of directions with students. For A, have students read the words aloud and then check known words.

## Sight Words

drive • rig • road

**A. Read the words above. Then read the sentence.**

I **drive** my **rig** down the **road**.

**B. Underline the new words in sentences 1–4.**

1. In my job I'm on the road day and night.

2. When I drive my rig, I have my CB radio on.

3. I talk to people like me who are on the road.

4. I'm lucky to own the rig I drive.

**Note:** The letters <u>d</u> and <u>r</u> go together to stand for the <u>dr</u> sound in the word <u>drive</u>.

**C. Write the letters in the order that makes a word.**

igr     _____

aodr    _____

viedr   _____

**D. Write the word that best completes each sentence.**

   drive     road     rig

1. There are no stores on this country _____ .

2. I'll have to _____ into the city to get food.

3. I worked for some time to buy my own _____ .

**E. Write your own sentence. Use one of the new words.**

_____

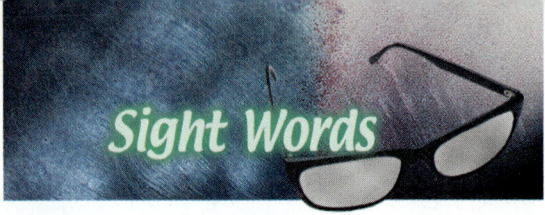

# Sight Words

**truck • heavy • carry**

**A. Read the words above. Then read the sentence.**

My **truck** is **heavy** and can **carry** a lot.

**Note:** The letters t and r go together to stand for the tr sound in truck and trouble.

**B. Underline the new words in sentences 1–4.**

1. The more I carry, the more money I can make.

2. This time my truck will carry heavy goods.

3. When I carry heavy goods, I need more time to get there.

4. It's a big job to drive a heavy truck.

**C. Look down and across. Find the words in the box. Circle them.**

truck

heavy

carry

| q | j | t | r | u | c | k |
|---|---|---|---|---|---|---|
| z | g | p | l | i | a | f |
| v | f | d | y | l | r | m |
| x | k | q | l | s | r | x |
| l | h | e | a | v | y | z |

**D. Write the word that best completes each sentence.**

**carry    heavy    truck**

1. My old friend Bill drives a _____ like mine.

2. Our rigs are fitted for _____ goods.

3. There are a lot of laws about what goods a rig can _____ .

**E. Write your own sentence. Use one of the new words.**

_____

**Instructor's Notes:** Read each set of directions with students. Read each sight word aloud and have students repeat it. Read the *tr* note in the box. Ask for other words that begin with *tr*.

76

Unit 6

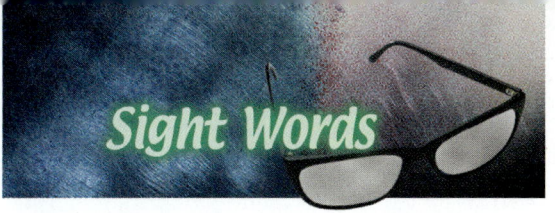

# Sight Words

cold • lonely • mind

**A. Read the words above. Then read the sentence.**

When I drive on a **cold**, **lonely** road, I have a lot on my **mind**.

**B. Underline the new words in sentences 1–4.**

1. On cold days like this, I get lonely.

2. On good days, I don't mind being on the road.

3. It's a lonely job to drive a heavy rig all day.

4. Hope and the children are on my mind.

**C. Write the three new words into the puzzle.**

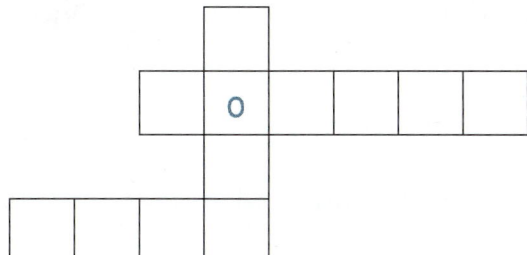

**D. Write the word that best completes each sentence.**

cold    lonely    mind

1. My _____ is with my family.

2. When it's _____ out, I want to be home.

3. Feeling _____ comes with the job.

**E. Write your own sentence. Use one of the new words.**

_____

**Instructor's Notes:** Read each set of directions with students. Read each sight word aloud and have students repeat it. Point out two meanings of *mind*: "thoughts" and "dislike."

## Phonics — Short i

**-ig**
rig
big
dig

**A. Read the words on the left. Write other -ig words.**

f + ig = _____

p + ig = _____

w + ig = _____

**B. Read the sentences. Circle the words with -ig. Write them.**

1. Some truckers carry pigs in from the country.

   _____

2. Can I learn to drive a heavy rig? _____

3. My son wants to drive a truck when he gets big.

   _____

**C. Look across. Find the new words. Mark out letters that do not belong in each new word.**

1. K R I G D
2. L X W I G
3. P I G Q L
4. Y D I G Z

**D. Write your own sentence. Use an -ig word.**

_____

_____

**Instructor's Notes:** Show students the -ig word pattern in the known sight word rig. Then read each set of directions with students. For A, tell students that the i stands for its short sound in these words.

# Long o

**-old**
cold
fold
old
sold

**A. Read the words on the left. Write other -old words.**

b + old = _____

g + old = _____

h + old = _____

m + old = _____

t + old = _____

**B. Read the sentences. Circle the words with -old. Write them.**

1. It's cold and lonely on the road. _____

2. I'll hold on to the job because it pays well. _____

3. I hope the rig won't be sold. _____

**C. Circle the word that fits best in each sentence.**

1. The truck I drive is red and (gold, hold).

2. The truck is set up to carry (bold, cold) foods.

3. The boss (fold, told) me to drive at night.

4. He (sold, gold) the food on the truck to a food store.

**D. Write your own sentence. Use an -old word.**

_____

_____

**Instructor's Notes:** Show students the *-old* word pattern in the known sight word *cold*. Then read each set of directions with students. For A, tell students that the letter *o* stands for the long vowel sound in these words. Note that these words do not end in silent *e*.

## Writing Skills

## Dropping Final e to Add -ed and -ing

hope + ed = hoped    hope + ing = hoping
Some words like hope end in e.
To add -ed or -ing to the word, drop the e.

**A. Drop the letter e. Add -ed and write the word. Then add -ing and write the word.**

1. fake _____ _____

2. like _____ _____

3. love _____ _____

4. time _____ _____

5. tune _____ _____

6. use _____ _____

**B. Practice reading the sentences. Circle the words with -ed and -ing.**

I loved trucks and cars when I was a child. I liked to be with my dad, and sometimes I used to drive with him to work. He had a job tuning up cars and vans. I learned from Dad about a car's timing. Today I'm a trucker, and I've used what I learned from Dad.

**C. Write one of these words in each sentence.**

tuning    loved    timing

1. I _____ trucks and cars when I was a child.

2. Dad had a job _____ up cars and vans.

3. I learned about a car's _____ from him.

**Instructor's Notes:** Read the examples and the explanation together. Read each set of directions with students. Have students read the -ed and -ing forms of each word aloud.

**D. Drop the e and add -ed. Write the new word in the sentence.**

1. use _____ I _____ a new truck.

2. hope _____ I _____ for more time.

3. like _____ Pam _____ my truck.

4. love _____ She _____ the holiday.

**E. Drop the e and add -ing. Write the new word in the sentence.**

1. time _____ The _____ is bad.

2. tune _____ I gave it a good _____ .

3. use _____ I'm _____ the new truck.

4. hope _____ I'm _____ to get home today.

**F. Use each word in a sentence of your own.**

1. using

   _____

2. hoped

   _____

3. liking

   _____

**Instructor's Notes:** Read each set of directions with students. Review the examples on page 80. For F, have students read sentences aloud.

Unit 6

**Back to the story...**

**Remember**
What has happened in the story so far?

**Predict**
Look at the picture. What do you think will happen in the rest of the story?

# A Life on the Go

Hope: It will feel good to give you a big hug when you get home, Dell. I get lonely for you, and I need help with the kids. Mike has a cold. Pam fell down and got a bad cut on her leg. I had to take her to the clinic. Can't you quit this trucking job and find work at home?

Dell: It's no fun having a job on the road, Hope. You and Mike and Pam are on my mind all the time. But people who drive heavy rigs make good money. I've told you that.

Mike: Hi, Dad! Things are OK, but I've got some problems. I got in a fight today because some kid said I was fat. Pam wants to play with me all the time, but I end up having to carry her. She gets heavy! When you come home, will you read to me about trucks?

Dell: I love reading to you, son. But don't tell me you want to drive a rig like I do. It gets cold and lonely on the road. Sometimes I don't get home in time for the holidays.

Hope: You can tell that Mike loves his dad! Mike told me he wants to have his own rig when he's bigger. But can my son cope with the life of a trucker?

Hope: The time you have at home does go by!

Dell: Being on the road all the time gets old. When the kids get bigger, maybe my sister will keep them from time to time. She's a lot of fun, and they like her. Then I can take you with me on the road. I love you, Hope. Having you with me will keep me from being lonely.

Hope: I wanted you to say that, Dell. It makes me feel good. I love you, and driving the rig will give us lots of time to talk. There is a big country out there to see. Down the road, there will be lots of love and no more lonely times.

## Comprehension

**Think About It**

1. Why does Dell keep in touch with his family?
2. What problems does Hope have to handle on her own?
3. How does Dell feel about his job? How do his wife and family feel about his job?
4. Sum up what happened in the story.

**Write About It**

Would you like "a life on the go"? Why or why not?

**Instructor's Notes:** Help students read and answer the questions. Write About It can be used as a writing or discussion assignment. Use the Unit 6 Review on page 85 to conclude the unit. Then assign *Reading for Today Workbook Three*, Unit 6.

## Unit 6 Review

**A. Complete each sentence. Use each word only once.**

> mind     lonely     road     truck     heavy     carry

1. I drive my _____ down the _____ .

2. My rig is _____ and can _____ a lot.

3. I can get _____ on the road.

4. I have a lot on my _____ .

**B. Write -ig or -old to make new words. Write the word that fits best in each sentence.**

1. r + _____ = _____    I drive a heavy _____ .

2. b + _____ = _____    I need a _____ truck.

3. c + _____ = _____    It's _____ and lonely sometimes.

4. s + _____ = _____    The rig will not be _____ .

**C. Add -ed and -ing to the words. Write the words on the lines below.**

1. like     _____     _____

2. love     _____     _____

3. smoke     _____     _____

4. tape     _____     _____

5. time     _____     _____

6. use     _____     _____

# Unit 7  Working Together for Change

## Discussion

**Remember**

Look at the picture. Is there a place in your neighborhood that could use some improvement?

**Predict**

Read the story title. What do you think the plan will be about? Why do you think the plan "grew"?

# The Plan That Grew

May: I used to like this street, but I don't feel very good about it today. Look at that lot!

Reed: You're right. It makes me sick. The lot isn't safe, and someone's going to get hurt there. I don't want my children playing there.

May: Did you know that the city owns this lot?

Reed: So, why doesn't the city fix it up?

May: Ha! The city has bigger problems.

Doc: You know, <u>we</u> can do something about the lot.

May: We can?

Reed: What?

*The story continues.*

**Instructor's Notes:** Read the discussion questions with students. Discuss the story title and the photo. Ask students to think of different meanings for the word *grew*. Have students read the page silently or read it aloud with them. Have students underline words they don't recognize. Review the underlined words. Have students identify the three people who are speaking.

## Review Words

**A. Check the words you don't know.**

- ☐ 1. about
- ☐ 2. children
- ☐ 3. weeds
- ☐ 4. hurt
- ☐ 5. what
- ☐ 6. someone
- ☐ 7. play
- ☐ 8. right
- ☐ 9. safe
- ☐ 10. own
- ☐ 11. there
- ☐ 12. problem

**B. Read and write the sentences. Circle the review words.**

1. Parents are upset because their children are not safe when they play in this lot.

   _____

2. Can you see all the glass and weeds there?

   _____

3. It's not right for the city to own the lot and let it be like this.

   _____

4. I hope someone can do something about the problem.

   _____

5. What can May do so no one gets hurt there?

   _____

**C. Write a sentence. Use a review word.**

_____

**Instructor's Notes:** Read each set of directions with students. For A, have students read the words aloud and then check known words. You might also have students find these words in the story on page 87.

# Sight Words

**camera** • **still**
**photo** • **garden**

**A. Read the words above. Then read the sentence.**

Hold the **camera still** when you take a **photo** of the **garden**.

**Note:** The letters <u>s</u> and <u>t</u> go together to stand for the <u>st</u> sound in the words <u>still</u>, <u>stop</u>, and <u>store</u>.

**B. Underline the new words in sentences 1–3.**

1. We'll use this camera to make photo records of the lot.

2. The photos will help the city see our problem.

3. Can we still plan a garden where the lot is?

**C. Look down and across. Find the words in the box. Circle them.**

camera
photo
garden
still

| g | a | r | d | e | n | c | s |
|---|---|---|---|---|---|---|---|
| b | s | g | x | q | i | l | t |
| q | c | a | m | e | r | a | i |
| n | p | h | o | t | o | i | l |
| p | k | f | d | v | z | a | l |

**D. Write the word that best completes each sentence.**

    **garden    camera    still    photos**

1. Where did you set the _____ you were using?

2. You set it down when you stopped taking _____ .

3. I bet Reed _____ has the camera.

4. We hope the city lets us have a _____ .

**Instructor's Notes:** Read each set of directions with students. Read each sight word aloud and have students repeat it. Explain that the *ph* in *photo* sounds like *f*. Read the *st* note. Ask for other words that begin with *st*.

# Sight Words

**street • drag • action**

**A. Read the words above. Then read the sentence.**

Will these photos of the **street** get some **action**, or do we have to **drag** someone who works for the city here?

**B. Underline the new words in sentences 1–3.**

1. This street sees a lot of action.

2. The lot at the end of the street is a big problem.

3. We need a plan so our talks with the city don't drag on and on.

**Note:** The letters <u>s</u>, <u>t</u>, and <u>r</u> go together to stand for the *str* sound in the word <u>street</u>.

**C. Write the three new words into the puzzle.**

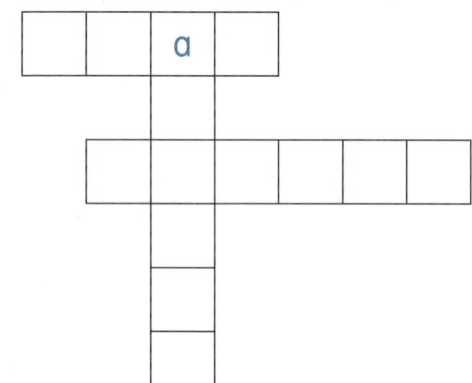

**D. Write the word that best completes each sentence.**

action    drag    street

1. People with homes on this _____ are upset.

2. People _____ old things to the lot and leave them there.

3. The home owners want to take _____ .

**E. Write your own sentence. Use one of the new words.**

_____

**Instructor's Notes:** Read each set of directions with students. Read each sight word aloud and have students repeat it. Read the *str* note in the box. Ask for other words that begin with *str*.

# Sight Words

**many • together • beat**

**A. Read the words above. Then read the sentence.**

When **many** people work **together**, they can **beat** a big problem.

**B. Underline the new words in sentences 1–4.**

1. Many people are upset about the lot.

2. We got together and talked.

3. We met with many city workers about our plan.

4. People can beat a problem if they work at it.

**C. Write the letters in the order that makes a word.**

ateb            _____

getherto        _____

yamn            _____

**D. Write the word that best completes each sentence.**

**many    beat    together**

1. We worked on our plan for _____ days.

2. We got _____ at different homes on the street.

3. We were _____ by the time we got it right.

**E. Write your own sentence. Use one of the new words.**

_____

**Instructor's Notes:** Read each set of directions with students. Read each sight word aloud and have students repeat it. Discuss the different meanings of *beat* in B and D.

91

Unit 7

# Phonics  Short a

**-ag**
drag
bag
rag
sag

**A. Read the words on the left. Write other -ag words.**

g + ag = _____

l + ag = _____

n + ag = _____

t + ag = _____

w + ag = _____

**B. Read the sentences. Circle the words with -ag. Write them.**

1. May has to carry her camera in a heavy bag.

   _____

2. She drags it with her all the time. _____

3. Sometimes she lags behind us to take photos of that lot.

   _____

4. Our group plans to nag the city to fix the lot.

   _____

**C. Look across. Find the new words. Mark out letters that do not belong in each new word.**

1. | Q | T | A | G | K |

2. | G | A | G | K | U |

3. | O | V | W | A | G |

4. | L | R | A | G | H |

**D. Write your own sentence. Use an -ag word.**

_____

**Instructor's Notes:** Show students the -ag word pattern in the known sight word *drag*. Then read each set of directions with students. For A, tell students that the words have the short *a* vowel sound. Review the *dr* sound in *drag*.

# Phonics

## Long e

**-eat**
beat
heat
neat
treat

**A. Read the words on the left. Write the other -eat words.**

f + eat = _____

s + eat = _____

m + eat = _____

wh + eat = _____

**B. Read the sentences. Circle the words with -eat. Write them.**

1. Reed will take a seat at City Hall to talk about the problem. _____

2. We need the lot to be neat and safe. _____

3. We can beat City Hall. We can't lose! _____

4. City Hall will have to treat us right. _____

**C. Circle the right word in each sentence.**

1. The weeds in the lot are as tall as (meat, wheat).

2. The sun (treats, beats) down on us all day.

3. The (heat, seat) can make you feel sick.

4. With a bit of work, we can make the lot look (feat, neat).

**D. Write your own sentence. Use an -eat word.**

_____

**Instructor's Notes:** Show students the -eat word pattern in the know sight word beat. Then read each set of directions with students. For A, tell students that the words have the long e vowel sound. Review the rule about vowels appearing in a word side by side. Review the tr sound in treat and the wh sound in wheat.

93

Unit 7

# Writing Skills  Quotation Marks

> 1. Put quotation marks (" ") before and after what a person says to show the words that are spoken.
> 2. Put a comma (,) between these quoted words and the rest of the sentence.
> 3. Begin the first word a person says with a capital letter.
>
> "Come see the photos," Reed said.
>
> May said, "The photos are in the *City Sun*."

### A. Practice reading the sentences.

"How about making a garden where the lot is?" asked Doc. "People on our street can grow things there."

May said, "I like that, Doc."

### B. Read the sentences. Then write them.

1. "A garden is a lot of work," said Vin.

   _____

2. Doc said, " I know, but it will be fun working together."

   _____

3. "Let's get the action going," said Reed.

   _____

### C. Read the sentences. Circle the quotation marks and commas.

1. "You can't beat a garden when it comes to making a street look good," said May.

2. "Get out your camera when the garden comes to life," said Doc.

3. Vin said, "You can bet I'll take photos of it!"

**Instructor's Notes:** Read the examples and the explanation together. Discuss the examples. Read each set of directions with students. Have students read the sentences in A, B, and C aloud to show the conversation of the speakers.

**D. Read each pair of sentences. Underline the one that is correct.**

1. Doc said, "People can fix up a street."

   Doc said "People can fix up a street."

2. We can make the lot look good, said May.

   "We can make the lot look good," said May.

3. "A garden will be a treat for us all," said Reed.

   "A garden will be a treat for us all, said Reed.

4. Vin said, "we can do this together."

   Vin said, "We can do this together."

**E. Write each sentence below. Write in quotation marks, commas, and capital letters.**

1. Doc said can i help you carry that heavy bag?

   _____

2. it isn't heavy to me said may.

   _____

3. let me use the camera to take a photo said reed.

   _____

**F. What might people say about your street? Write three sentences using quotation marks.**

1. _____

2. _____

3. _____

**Instructor's Notes:** Read each set of directions with students. For F, discuss possible quotations and help students write their sentences.

> **Back to the story...**
>
> **Remember**
> What has happened in the story so far?
>
> **Predict**
> Look at the picture. What do you think will happen in the rest of the story?

# The Plan That Grew

Many people on Ninth Street wanted to take action about the lot. They wanted to make it into a garden for all the people on the street to use.

"The city has money for gardens like this if people have good plans," said Doc. "Let's go for it!" So people met at Doc's home. They worked together on teams. May's group got cameras to take photos of the old lot.

"We'll send the photos," said May. "That way people who work for the city can see what a big job we have and how needed it is!"

Doc's group worked on the garden plans. They talked about what to grow and they made a map. Reed's group looked into buying things like seeds and rakes that they would need.

The Ninth Street gardeners were upbeat when they sent their plan to the city. They hoped to sell the city on their garden because they needed money to get going. Many days went by. What would the city do?

On the seventh day, a worker from the city asked people from the group to come and talk to her. Reed, May, and Doc went to see her.

"You have a very good plan," said Ann. "The city likes to help people like the Ninth Street gardeners. We will give you money to make a garden out of the lot. I hope the money will be well spent."

That June the people on Ninth Street worked in the lot. They got rid of loads of things—boxes, pots, logs, an old safe, a cot, bits of cars and trucks. They dragged in bags of seeds. They dug holes and covered and watered the seeds. Many children wanted to be in on the action. They asked for their own plot.

In no time the garden came to life. Some people were growing beets. There was an apple tree by the walk. A plum tree grew by a garden seat. The gate was covered by a vine. Life was good on Ninth Street. The garden looked fine. Many people made friends working together in the heat of the day. At night, when it was still, they sat and talked.

"Let's have a holiday," said Nan one day. "We'll sell the things we grew and make money for more seeds."

So they did. The gardeners set up big tables with umbrellas. People came to buy. A man from the *City Sun* took photos of the garden, the food, the action, and all the people.

"This is one neat garden," he said, "and one together street. Our readers will love this story. I bet more people will want gardens in the lots on their streets!"

## Comprehension

**Think About It**

1. What did the people on Ninth Street do about their lot?
2. What steps did they have to take?
3. How did the garden change things?
4. Sum up what happened in the story.

**Write About It**

What problems are there in your neighborhood? What could you do to help them?

**Instructor's Notes:** Help students read and answer the questions. Write About It can be used as a writing or discussion assignment. Use the Unit 7 Review on page 99 to conclude the unit. Then assign *Reading for Today Workbook Three*, Unit 7. Use Blackline Master 8: Certificate of Completion from the *Instructor's Guide* when students have successfully completed this book.

# Unit 7 Review

**A. Complete each sentence. Use each word only once.**

> photos   camera   street   beat   many   together

1. My _____ is in the heavy bag.

2. _____ people on this _____ want to take action.

3. People worked in the garden _____ .

4. Reed still takes lots of _____ of it.

**B. Write -ag or -eat to make new words. Write the word that fits best in each sentence.**

1. b + _____ = _____ The man had a big _____ of seeds.

2. t + _____ = _____ The children play _____ in the street.

3. h + _____ = _____ We all worked in the _____ .

4. s + _____ = _____ There is a _____ in the garden.

**C. Write each sentence. Add quotation marks, commas, and capital letters.**

1. we can help sell the food said the children.

   _____

2. May said these are heavy bags of beets.

   _____

3. you have to take a photo of the garden said reed.

   _____

99

Unit 7

# At Your Leisure

*Read pg. 100-101*
*pg. 102 A, B,*
*pg. 103 D, E*
*pg. 104 F, G-dictate*
*pg. 105 I, J, K  H-" "*
*Use word list on*
*pg. 122 and 123 to*
*work on pronunciation*

## Until I Saw the Sea

Until I saw the sea
I did not know
that wind could wrinkle water so.

I never knew
that sun
could splinter a whole sea of blue.

Nor
did I know before,
a sea breathes in and out
upon a shore.

*by Lilian Moore*

### What Do You Think?

**Have you ever seen the sea or a mountain or something else that made a strong impression on you?**

# The Amazing Sea

The sea is an amazing place. Do you think you know much about it? Here are some interesting facts.

**How big is the sea?**

The sea covers over 70 percent of the earth's surface. The sea holds 97 percent of the earth's water.

**How deep is the sea?**

The bottom of the Mariana Trench, a kind of valley in the sea floor, is 36,198 feet below sea level. If you set Mount Everest in the bottom of the trench, it wouldn't reach the surface.

**What is the sea floor like?**

Under the sea's surface is a mountain range called the mid-ocean ridges. The mountain range is 37,000 meters long and crosses three oceans. Some peaks of the mid-ocean ridges form islands.

Seamounts also rise from the ocean floor. Seamounts are formed by undersea volcanoes. They can be up to 13,000 feet tall.

**How big are ocean waves?**

Hurricanes cause the largest waves in the sea. They can be more than 100 feet high.

**What is the biggest animal in the sea?**

The biggest animal in the sea is the blue whale. Blue whales can grow to 100 feet long.

# Final Review

**A. Write the word that best completes each sentence.**

| see | hug | fine | parents |
|---|---|---|---|
| give | when | video | tapes |

1. I can't carry these _____ .

2. Will you _____ me some help?

3. This _____ sells well.

4. Did you _____ the name on it?

5. They are _____ players.

6. I saw them _____ they played in person.

**B. Write -ell, -ake, -ug, or -ine to make new words. Write the word in each sentence.**

1. t + _____ = _____   Will you _____ me to the store?

2. s + _____ = _____   They _____ tapes and CDs.

3. n + _____ = _____   I want to buy _____ tapes.

4. m + _____ = _____   This record is _____ .

5. r + _____ = _____   Why is it on the _____ ?

**C. Write two sentences of your own.**

1. A sentence that separates words in a series.

   _____

2. A sentence that starts with an introductory word.

   _____

102

**D. Write the word that fits best in each sentence.**

| upset | people | downhill |
|---|---|---|
| sometimes | children | leaves |

1. The _____ run to their mother.

2. They are _____ by the dog.

3. A dog can _____ nip you.

4. The _____ let the children pet the dog.

5. The dog ran _____ .

6. It played in the _____ .

**E. Write the word that fits best in each sentence.**

| uniform | day | team | problem |
|---|---|---|---|
| there | what | said | need |

1. Our _____ will play a night game.

2. I work all _____ .

3. I have to get my _____ .

4. That is my _____ .

5. I _____ to go home for it.

6. Is _____ someone with a car?

F. Write -ip, -ope, -ay, or -eed to make new words. Write the word that fits best in each sentence.

1. h + _____ = _____    I _____ this is pay day.

2. n + _____ = _____    I _____ the money.

3. t + _____ = _____    No one gave me a big _____.

4. c + _____ = _____    I _____ with a big job.

5. pl + _____ = _____    I need time to _____.

G. Write each sentence. Add quotation marks, commas, and capital letters.

1. i can help you with this garden said Will.

   _____

2. rose said you can carry this heavy load for me.

   _____

3. no problem said will.

   _____

H. Circle the commas and underline the words that end in -er. Write the sentence.

1. He is a helper, a reader, and a good worker.

   _____

2. Yes, he is a player on our team.

   _____

3. He stopped being a smoker on June 8, 2000.

   _____

104

**I. Write the word that fits best in each sentence. Use each word only once.**

| team | teach | right | different |
|------|-------|-------|-----------|
| carry | drive | truck | together |

1. Sam and I work _____ at the store.

2. We _____ boxes to the _____ .

3. Then we _____ to the city.

4. Our _____ does it _____ .

5. We _____ people to work with us.

**J. Write -ight, -une, -ute, -ig, or -old to make new words. Write the word that fits best in each sentence.**

1. c + _____ = _____    That's a _____ cat.

2. J + _____ = _____    Her name is _____ .

3. t + _____ = _____    She _____ me to feed her.

4. n + _____ = _____    She is up all _____ .

5. b + _____ = _____    She looks for _____ rats.

**K. Circle the word that fits best in each sentence.**

1. The camera is in the (bag, sag).

2. Nothing can (neat, beat) a good photo!

3. Take a (heat, seat) right there.

4. I will (wag, nag) you to sit still.

# Unit 1

## Page 4

A. Answers will vary.

B. 1. Max has (trouble) with his (music) store.
   2. (Some) of the (goods) in the store are (old).
   3. Max likes to fix (old) (guitars).
   4. Max (won't) (quit), but it's (time) for him to get (some) (help).
   5. Will Max find a (plan), or will he (lose) money?

C. Discuss your sentence with your instructor.

## Page 5

B. 1. When people stop by the store, they don't <u>see</u> <u>tapes</u> for sale.
   2. Max can <u>sell</u> <u>tapes</u> in his music store.
   3. He can make bigger sales with <u>tapes</u>.
   4. Will Max <u>see</u> that <u>tapes</u> can help the store?

C.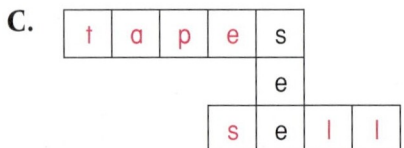

D. 1. sell   2. tape   3. see

E. Discuss your sentence with your instructor.

## Page 6

B. 1. Max has a lot of old <u>records</u> in the <u>shop</u>.
   2. We can sell the <u>records</u> for a quarter.
   3. I'll help out in Max's <u>shop</u> from time to time.
   4. It will <u>take</u> time to make the <u>shop</u> look good.

C.

| h | r | e | c | o | r | d | s |
| s | v | t | b | d | l | g | h |
| u | y | t | a | k | e | f | o |
| a | j | i | q | t | m | z | p |

D. 1. record   2. shop   3. take

E. Discuss your sentence with your instructor.

## Page 7

B. 1. Sales are <u>down</u> in Max's store.
   2. I'll talk to him about the <u>value</u> of selling <u>videos</u>.
   3. He can both rent and sell <u>videos</u> at the shop.
   4. Max will see the <u>value</u> in this plan.

C. value, down, video

D. 1. down   2. videos   3. value

E. Discuss your sentence with your instructor.

## Page 8

A. bell, Dell, Nell, yell

B. 1. Max's music shop was not doing (well).
   2. Can you see why the store (fell) on bad times?
   3. What is Max going to (sell) in his store?
   4. (Tell) some friends to stop by the store.

C. 1. ☒ Y E L L ☒ ☒
   2. ☒ ☒ W E L L ☒
   3. ☒ ☒ ☒ B E L L
   4. ☒ F E L L ☒ ☒

D. Discuss your sentence with your instructor.

## Page 9

A. bake, lake, rake, wake

106

B. 1. Max did take a good look at his shop.
   2. He can make money selling videos.
   3. Max had to wake up to what people are buying.
   4. I am helping out for Max's sake.

C. 1. make  2. sake  3. take  4. rake

D. Discuss your sentence with your instructor.

**Page 10**

A. 1. sailboat  2. sometimes  3. downhill
   4. baseball  5. goldfish

B. 1. home — cake
   2. skate — board
   3. pan — sick
   4. band — stand
   5. some — one

C. 1. base, ball
   2. work, out
   3. sea, sick
   4. tea, cup
   5. down, hill
   6. news, paper

**Page 11**

D. downhill, newspaper, sometimes, videotapes, workout

E. videotapes, tabletop, workout, baseball, goldfish

F. Discuss your sentences with your instructor.

**Page 14**

Think About It

Discuss your answers with your instructor.

1. Max didn't have up-to-date products in his store.
2. He began to sell videos, CDs, and tapes.
3. The store began to make money when customers rented and bought the new tapes, CDs, and videos.
4. Summaries should include the idea that Max did not want to change his store at first. Later, with his brother's help and friends' money, he did change his store, and it became a healthy business again.

Write About It

Discuss your writing with your instructor.

## Unit 1 Review

**Page 15**

A. 1. sells, records *or* tapes  2. tapes *or* records
   3. down  4. value

B. 1. sell *or* sake, sell
   2. well *or* wake, well
   3. tell *or* take, take
   4. make, make

C. 1. sometimes  2. upset  3. downhill
   4. workout  5. videotapes

# Unit 2

**Page 18**

A. Answers will vary.

B. 1. My brother and I went from home to home.
   2. Some children end up in a bad home.
   3. I feel like Nell and Bill are my mother and father.

107

4. They had time to talk and (laugh) with us.

5. At this (age) I can see that I was (lucky) to (find) (them).

C. Discuss your sentence with your instructor.

**Page 19**

B. 1. Some people don't have children, but they can be <u>parents</u>.

2. They are people <u>who</u> have love to <u>give</u>.

3. They take in children <u>who</u> don't have <u>parents</u>.

4. They <u>give</u> the children food, love, and a good home.

C.

| b | f | u | g | w | h | o |
|---|---|---|---|---|---|---|
| k | e | w | i | m | j | q |
| h | o | c | v | r | l | d |
| p | a | r | e | n | t | s |

D. 1. who   2. parents   3. give

E. Discuss your sentence with your instructor.

**Page 20**

B. 1. My father was in <u>fine</u> health, but he got sick.

2. Mother had a lot of trouble in her <u>life</u>.

3. Her <u>own</u> parents didn't love her.

4. Mother's <u>life</u> wasn't good, but she didn't give up.

C.

D. 1. life   2. fine   3. own

E. Discuss your sentence with your instructor.

**Page 21**

B. 1. <u>When</u> my father got sick, he had to give up his job.

2. The <u>social</u> <u>worker</u> had to find us a home.

3. Dad gave Ed and me a big <u>hug</u> <u>when</u> we went.

4. The <u>social</u> <u>worker</u> helped us find Bill and Nell.

C. hug, social worker, when

D. 1. social worker   2. when   3. hugs

E. Discuss your sentence with your instructor.

**Page 22**

A. jug, lug, mug, tug

B. 1. We got a (jug) of water to take with us.

2. We have an old (rug) to sit down on.

3. I bet the (bugs) will bite us.

4. The car (dug) a hole in the wet sand.

C. 1. X̸ L U G K̸
   2. T U G K X̸
   3. X̸ B K̸ U G
   4. K̸ H U G H̸

D. Discuss your sentence with your instructor.

**Page 23**

A. dine, mine, pine, vine, whine

B. 1. When I was (nine), Nell let me get a dog.

2. We had a (fine) time playing games.

3. All dogs (whine) from time to time.

4. Owners have to learn to keep a dog in (line).

C. 1. shine   2. mine   3. dine   4. pine

D. Discuss your sentence with your instructor.

## Page 24

A. women, lives, leaves, feet, men, people

B. 1. <u>Lots</u> of <u>men</u> are good <u>brothers</u>.

  2. Jean's father hurt his <u>feet</u>.

  3. Some <u>women</u> are <u>nurses</u>.

  4. My <u>sisters</u> had good <u>lives</u>.

C. Ed and I have had trouble in our (lives.) (We) are lucky that (social workers) helped (us.) (We) met (men) and (women) who loved (us) and gave (us) good (homes.)

  (Children) without good (parents) can give up on life. With help from (people) who give (them) a chance, (kids) can do well.

## Page 25

D. 1. mouse — people
  2. person — men
  3. child — leaves
  4. woman — socks
  5. sock — buses
  6. leaf — mice
  7. man — children
  8. bus — women

E. 1. Women   2. men
  3. children   4. feet

F. Discuss your sentences with your instructor.

## Page 28

### Think About It

Discuss your answers with your instructor.

1. They didn't have parents and lived in many different homes.

2. Answers will vary.

3. She learned the value of a good family, and that having good parents gives a child a chance to do well in life.

4. Summaries should include the idea that the girl had a rough childhood, had a set of loving foster parents, and had the determination to succeed on her own.

### Write About It

Discuss your writing with your instructor.

## Unit 2 Review

### Page 29

A. 1. parents, give
  2. own, life
  3. social worker
  4. hug, when

B. 1. hug, hug
  2. rug, rug
  3. fine, fine
  4. nine, nine

C. 1. woman   2. children
  3. These   4. men

# Unit 3

### Page 32

A. Answers will vary.

B. 1. When a mother (smokes,) she takes a (chance) with her child's (health.)

  2. Our (social worker) can get (glasses) for people who don't have money.

109

3. A (nurse) (talks) to (groups) (about) family (health.)

4. When I eat well, I feel (fine.)

5. I have to quit (smoking,) (but) I can't give it up.

C. Discuss your sentence with your instructor.

## Page 33

B. 1. At a good <u>clinic</u>, all who walk in get help.

2. People <u>hope</u> the <u>doctor</u> can tell them what to do.

3. At the <u>clinic</u>, the <u>doctor</u> helps people get well.

C.

|   |   |   | d |   |
|---|---|---|---|---|
|   |   |   | o |   |
| c | l | i | n | i | c |
|   |   |   | t |   |
|   |   | h | o | p | e |
|   |   |   | r |   |

D. 1. doctor   2. clinic   3. hopes

E. Discuss your sentence with your instructor.

## Page 34

B. 1. The woman <u>said</u> her hand wasn't mending.

2. <u>What</u> can she do about this <u>problem</u>?

3. The nurse can tell the woman <u>what</u> to do.

4. The nurse can help her work on the <u>problem</u>.

C. said, problem, what

D. 1. problems   2. what   3. said

E. Discuss your sentence with your instructor.

## Page 35

B. 1. Nan <u>wants</u> to see the doctor about her <u>hip</u>.

2. Standing and sitting makes her <u>hip</u> feel bad.

3. The doctor <u>wants</u> Nan to walk <u>more</u>.

4. He said <u>more</u> walking is good for her <u>hip</u>.

C.

| r | m | c | g | e | v | w |
| z | o | w | a | n | t | b |
| s | r | d | h | i | p | l |
| k | e | f | y | u | w | q |
| c | h | j | k | e | b | x |

D. 1. hip   2. want   3. more

E. Discuss your sentence with your instructor.

## Page 36

A. dip, nip, rip, zip

B. 1. The nurse has lots of health (tips.)

2. When the child fell down, he cut his (lip.)

3. A (sip) of cold water will help.

C. 1. ~~T~~ N I P ~~X~~   nip or tip
2. ~~E~~ C L I P   lip or clip
3. ~~T~~ M R I P   tip or rip
4. S H I P ~~X~~   hip or ship
5. ~~G~~ ~~X~~ Z I P   zip

D. Discuss your sentence with your instructor.

## Page 37

A. lope, mope, pope

B. 1. Jan feels that she has no (hope) of getting well.

2. She sits at home and (mopes) about her problems.

110

3. Jan can't (cope) with bad health.
4. I (hope) that Jan will get well.

C. 1. cope    2. rope

D. Discuss your sentence with your instructor.

## Page 38

A. 1. buyer    2. helper    3. reader
   4. smoker    5. talker    6. player

B. Ned Cutman was a <u>smoker</u>. When he quit, he wanted to be a <u>helper</u> at the health clinic. Sometimes he helps with the children. Ned is a good <u>reader</u>. He is a big <u>talker</u>. He is the one <u>worker</u> who makes the children laugh. He is a big <u>seller</u> of good health.

C. 1. talker — own
   2. buyer — smoke
   3. smoker — make
   4. owner — talk
   5. maker — buy

## Page 39

D. 1. teller    2. walker    3. faker
   4. seller    5. shaker    6. payer

E. 1. smoker    2. helper *or* worker
   3. reader    4. talker
   5. helper *or* worker

Note: Most of these words fit in most of the sentences. Any reasonable answer is correct.

F. Discuss your sentences with your instructor.

## Page 42

Think About It

Discuss your answers with your instructor.

1. The doctor treats patients. She works with nurses and social workers, and she keeps a daily log.

2. The doctor uses a daily log as a record of clinic work and daily problems.

3. Answers will vary.

4. Summaries should include the idea that the doctor treats patients for physical problems, refers some patients to self-help groups or social services, and works with social workers and with patients' families.

Write About It

Discuss your writing with your instructor.

## Unit 3 Review

### Page 43

A. 1. doctor, clinic    2. said
   3. hope    4. hip

B. 1. hip *or* hope, hip
   2. tip, tip
   3. hope *or* hip, hope
   4. cope, cope

C. 1. helper    2. player    3. worker
   4. smoker    5. reader

## Unit 4

### Page 46

A. Answers will vary.

B. 1. The (boss) likes our (work.)
   2. We (hope) Jake will be a (helper.)
   3. Jake doesn't (lend) a (hand) at the (store.)
   4. Will Jan (see) the (trouble) we have?

5. Jan (asked) about the (problem.)

C. Discuss your sentence with your instructor.

**Page 47**

B. 1. Ray and I are a <u>team</u>.

2. We <u>need</u> a third man.

3. Jan sees what we <u>need</u>.

4. Can Jake <u>load</u> from 7:00 to 3:00?

C. team    need    load

D. 1. load    2. need    3. team

E. Discuss your sentence with your instructor.

**Page 48**

B. 1. The <u>uniform</u> has a name on it.

2. Jake feels the <u>uniform</u> <u>does</u> not fit him.

3. The <u>day</u> <u>does</u> not go well.

4. A <u>day</u> like this upsets Ray and me.

C.
| u | n | i | f | o | r | m |
|---|---|---|---|---|---|---|
| d | a | y | l | m | p | l |
| o | r | s | l | t | x | r |
| e | n | f | b | g | u | v |
| s | h | j | d | c | r | x |

D. 1. uniform    2. does    3. day

E. Discuss your sentence with your instructor.

**Page 49**

B. 1. We have to <u>cover</u> the boxes.

2. We do it <u>because</u> that's our job.

3. Are <u>there</u> more boxes in the store?

C.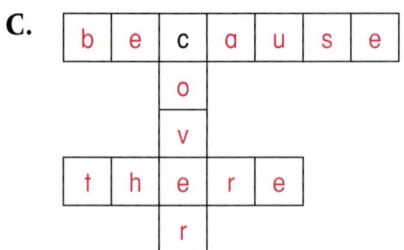

D. 1. because    2. there    3. cover

E. Discuss your sentence with your instructor.

**Page 50**

A. hay, Jay, lay, ray, say

B. 1. Jake (may) not fit our team.

2. (Ray) and I don't like the (way) he works!

3. One (day,) we will (say) this to Jan.

4. She will not (pay) Jake for bad work.

C. 1. ⊠ H A Y ⊠ ⊠    hay
   2. R ⊠ P A Y ⊠    pay
   3. ⊠ ⊠ ⊠ S A Y    say
   4. J A Y ⊠ ⊠ ⊠    jay
   5. ⊠ C L A Y ⊠    clay

D. Discuss your sentence with your instructor.

**Page 51**

A. reed, seed, weed

B. 1. Jake does not help Ray load (seed) at the store.

2. Ray and I (need) to talk to Jan about this.

3. That will be a good (deed) for our boss.

4. Jan (needs) to (weed) out problems at work.

C. 1. weeds    2. need    3. feed    4. Heed

D. Discuss your sentences with your instructor.

## Page 52

**A.** Students' sentences should include commas as shown in 1–6.

## Page 53

**B.**
1. I work, do my job, and get my pay.
2. Jake, what is your problem?
3. It was June 6, 2000.
4. Jake sat, looked, and didn't help.

**C.**
1. I work, help, and laugh with Ray.
2. It is May 8, 2000.
3. Ray, are you mad at Jake?

**D.** Discuss your sentences with your instructor.

## Page 56

Think About It

Discuss your answers with your instructor.

1. Jake didn't help them work.
2. Tip 1: Don't get mad. Tip 2: Talk about the job, not about people. Tip 3: Listen to the other person. Tip 4: Make a plan together.
3. He didn't know how to help or how he fit on the team.
4. Summaries should include the idea that Ray and Sam needed help. Their boss, Jan, agreed. Jake was hired, but he sat around and didn't help. Ray and Sam asked Jan what to do. She gave them four tips for working together as a team. They used the tips, and Jake became a good team member.

Write About It

Discuss your writing with your instructor.

# Unit 4 Review

## Page 57

**A.**
1. The day went well <u>because</u> we worked like a team.
2. He does not like his red <u>uniform</u>.
3. We need to <u>load</u> the boxes into the van.
4. Is <u>there</u> a cover for this box of records?

**B.**
1. need, need
2. way *or* weed, way
3. play, play
4. hay *or* heed, heed

**C.**
1. Jake, can you help?
2. It is June 8, 2000.
3. Yes, he's here.
4. Jake, Ray, and Sam are a team.

# Unit 5

## Page 60

**A.** Answers will vary.

**B.**
1. (My) (dog) wants to (do) well, but sometimes he makes (mistakes.)
2. (His) (eyes) shine with pride when he (does) well.
3. Sundown likes to (eat,) and he will (be) (fed) two times a day.
4. (Did) Sundown (eat) all (his) food?
5. I (send) (my) (dog) out to play when (his) work ends.

**C.** Discuss your sentence with your instructor.

## Page 61

**B.**
1. Not all <u>prisons</u> give people a chance like this.

113

2. The dogs we teach will help people someday.
3. The dogs learn to work with people who need them.
4. I hope I can use this prison job when I get out.

C.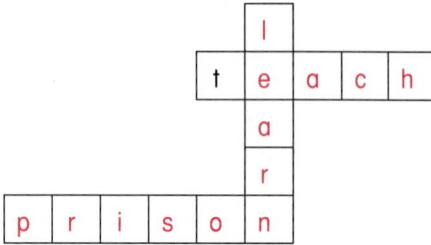

D. 1. teach   2. learning   3. prison
E. Discuss your sentence with your instructor.

## Page 62

B. 1. We teach our dogs to do different things.
2. These dogs are helpers for disabled people.
3. People have different needs for our dogs.
4. Dogs help disabled people to get out.

C. disabled, things, different
D. 1. different, things   2. disabled
E. Discuss your sentence with your instructor.

## Page 63

B. 1. June had to learn to work with her dog.
2. She learned the right way to tell the dog what to do.
3. The dog comes when June calls it.
4. June has the right dog for her needs.

C.

| s | w | d | a | l | c | n |
| f | l | p | c | k | o | y |
| r | i | g | h | t | m | b |
| a | k | j | u | n | e | x |
| z | q | b | f | p | d | v |

D. 1. right   2. June   3. come
E. Discuss your sentence with your instructor.

## Page 64

A. light, might, tight
B. 1. Our dogs help people with bad sight.
2. They are on the job day and night.
3. Disabled people need to find a dog that is right for them.

C. 1. ⊠ F I G H T ⊠
2. ⊠ ⊠ M I G H T
3. L I G H T ⊠ ⊠
4. ⊠ T I G H T ⊠
5. ⊠ ⊠ N I G H T

D. Discuss your sentence with your instructor.

## Page 65

A. cute, lute, mute
B. 1. Some disabled people can't talk. They are mute.
2. June has trouble getting about in the city because she can't see.
3. Her dog may be cute, but it isn't a pet.

C. 1. tune   2. dunes   3. mute   4. cute
D. Discuss your sentence with your instructor.

## Page 66

**A.** came, said, knew, were, went, took, gave, fed

**B.** I (came) to this prison to do time. Some of the prisoners (were) working with dogs. One day I (went) to see them. They (gave) me a dog to work with. Working with Sundown (took) a lot of time, but helping out (gave) me a good feeling.

**C.** 1. fed  2. grew  3. knew  4. said

## Page 67

**D.** 1. were  2. took  3. went
    4. came  5. said  6. gave

**E.** 1. present  2. past  3. past  4. present

**F.** Discuss your sentences with your instructor.

## Page 70

<u>Think About It</u>

Discuss your answers with your instructor.

1. She learned to train dogs to help disabled people.
2. She grows to love them and is sad to see them go.
3. June's life became better when she got Sundown. He helped her become more independent.
4. Summaries should include the idea that Fay put her prison time to good use, and became more hopeful about her future. They may also include the idea that June became more hopeful about her future after she got Sundown.

<u>Write About It</u>

Discuss your writing with your instructor.

## Unit 5 Review

### Page 71

**A.** 1. learn  2. come
    3. disabled  4. different

**B.** 1. might, might  2. sight, sight
    3. fight, fight  4. June, June

**C.** 1. come — did
    2. do — were
    3. is — went
    4. are — came
    5. go — was

(matching: come–came, do–did, is–was, are–were, go–went)

## Unit 6

### Page 74

**A.** Answers will vary.

**B.** 1. I (bet) I won't make it home (on) the (holidays.)
    2. My (son) (will) be (upset) about that.
    3. I (bet) a job with a (bigger) store (will) (fit) my needs.
    4. I (read) the (ads,) but there are (no) jobs for someone like me.
    5. Maybe my friend Bill (will) give me a (hand.)

**C.** Discuss your sentence with your instructor.

### Page 75

**B.** 1. In my job I'm on the <u>road</u> day and night.
    2. When I <u>drive</u> my <u>rig</u>, I have my CB radio on.
    3. I talk to people like me who are on the <u>road</u>.
    4. I'm lucky to own the <u>rig</u> I <u>drive</u>.

C. rig, road, drive

D. 1. road   2. drive   3. rig

E. Discuss your sentence with your instructor.

## Page 76

B. 1. The more I carry, the more money I can make.

2. This time my truck will carry heavy goods.

3. When I carry heavy goods, I need more time to get there.

4. It's a big job to drive a heavy truck.

C. 
| q | j | t | r | u | c | k |
|---|---|---|---|---|---|---|
| z | g | p | l | i | a | f |
| v | f | d | y | l | r | m |
| x | k | q | l | s | r | x |
| l | h | e | a | v | y | z |

D. 1. truck   2. heavy   3. carry

E. Discuss your sentence with your instructor.

## Page 77

B. 1. On cold days like this, I get lonely.

2. On good days, I don't mind being on the road.

3. It's a lonely job to drive a heavy rig all day.

4. Hope and the children are on my mind.

C.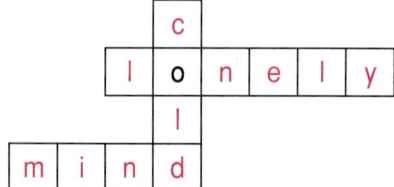

D. 1. mind   2. cold   3. lonely

E. Discuss your sentence with your instructor.

## Page 78

A. fig, pig, wig

B. 1. Some truckers carry pigs in from the country.

2. Can I learn to drive a heavy rig?

3. My son wants to drive a truck when he gets big.

C. 1. K̶ R I G X̶
   2. X̶ X̶ W I G
   3. P I G X̶ X̶
   4. X̶ D I G X̶

D. Discuss your sentence with your instructor.

## Page 79

A. bold, gold, hold, mold, told

B. 1. It's cold and lonely on the road.

2. I'll hold on to the job because it pays well.

3. I hope the rig won't be sold.

C. 1. gold   2. cold   3. told   4. sold

D. Discuss your sentence with your instructor.

## Page 80

A. 1. faked, faking
   2. liked, liking
   3. loved, loving
   4. timed, timing
   5. tuned, tuning
   6. used, using

B. I loved trucks and cars when I was a child. I liked to be with my dad, and sometimes I used to drive with him to work. He had a job tuning up cars and vans. I learned from Dad about a car's timing. Today I'm

116

a trucker, and I've (used) what I (learned) from Dad.

C. 1. loved   2. tuning   3. timing

## Page 81

D. 1. used   2. hoped   3. liked   4. loved

E. 1. timing   2. tuning   3. using   4. hoping

F. Discuss your sentences with your instructor.

## Page 84

Think About It

Discuss your answers with your instructor.

1. He misses them and wants to get news from home.

2. She has to handle the children's illnesses, accidents, and general care.

3. Dell likes making good money, but sometimes feels lonely. His family wishes he worked closer to home.

4. Summaries should include the idea that Dell and Hope dislike being separated so much, but they both accept Dell's way of making a living.

Write About It

Discuss your writing with your instructor.

## Unit 6 Review

## Page 85

A. 1. truck, road
   2. heavy, carry
   3. lonely
   4. mind

B. 1. rig, rig
   2. big *or* bold, big

3. cold, cold
4. sold, sold

C. 1. liked, liking
   2. loved, loving
   3. smoked, smoking
   4. taped, taping
   5. timed, timing
   6. used, using

# Unit 7

## Page 88

A. Answers will vary.

B. 1. Parents are upset because their (children) are not (safe) when they (play) in this lot.

2. Can you see all the glass and (weeds) (there)?

3. It's not (right) for the city to (own) the lot and let it be like this.

4. I hope (someone) can do something (about) the (problem).

5. (What) can May do so no one gets (hurt) (there)?

C. Discuss your sentence with your instructor.

## Page 89

B. 1. We'll use this <u>camera</u> to make <u>photo</u> records of the lot.

2. The <u>photos</u> will help the city see the problem.

3. Can we <u>still</u> plan a <u>garden</u> where the lot is?

C.

| g | a | r | d | e | n | c | s |
|---|---|---|---|---|---|---|---|
| b | s | g | x | q | i | l | t |
| q | c | a | m | e | r | a | i |
| n | p | h | o | t | o | i | l |
| p | k | f | d | v | z | a | l |

D. 1. camera  2. photos  3. still  4. garden

## Page 90

B. 1. This <u>street</u> sees a lot of <u>action</u>.

2. The lot at the end of the <u>street</u> is a big problem.

3. We need a plan so our talks with the city don't <u>drag</u> on and on.

C.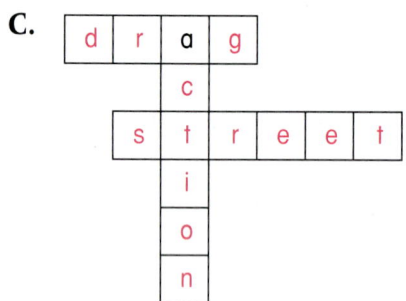

D. 1. street   2. drag   3. action

E. Discuss your sentence with your instructor.

## Page 91

B. 1. <u>Many</u> people are upset about the lot.

2. We got <u>together</u> and talked.

3. We met with <u>many</u> city workers about our plan.

4. People can <u>beat</u> a problem if they work at it.

C. beat, together, many

D. 1. many   2. together   3. beat

E. Discuss your sentence with your instructor.

## Page 92

A. gag, lag, nag, tag, wag

B. 1. May has to carry her camera in a heavy (bag).

2. She (drags) it with her all the time.

3. Sometimes she (lags) behind us to take photos of that lot.

4. Our group plans to (nag) the city to fix the lot.

C. 1. ~~B~~  T  A  G  K
   2. G  A  G  K  ~~N~~
   3. ~~B~~  ~~N~~  W  A  G
   4. ~~L~~  R  A  G  ~~N~~

D. Discuss your sentence with your instructor.

## Page 93

A. feat, seat, meat, wheat

B. 1. Reed will take a (seat) at City Hall to talk about the problem.

2. We need the lot to be (neat) and safe.

3. We can (beat) City Hall. We can't lose!

4. City Hall will have to (treat) us right.

C. 1. wheat   2. beats   3. heat   4. neat

D. Discuss your sentence with your instructor.

## Page 94

B. 1. "A garden is a lot of work," said Vin.

2. Doc said, "I know, but it will be fun working together."

3. "Let's get the action going," said Reed.

C. 1. "You can't beat a garden when it comes to making a street look good," said May.

118

2. "Get out your camera when the garden comes to life," said Doc.

3. Vin said, "You can bet that I'll take photos of it."

**Page 95**

D. 1. Doc said, "People can fix up a street."

2. "We can make the lot look good," said May.

3. "A garden will be a treat for us all," said Reed.

4. Vin said, "We can do this together."

E. 1. Doc said, "Can I help you carry that heavy bag?"

2. "It isn't heavy to me," said May.

3. "Let me use the camera to take a photo," said Reed.

F. Discuss your sentences with your instructor.

**Page 98**

Think About It

Discuss your answers with your instructor.

1. They made it into a community garden.

2. They drew up a plan, submitted it to the city, got approval, then went to work.

3. It helped people become friends as they worked together, and it improved the street, providing a nice place to sit and talk.

4. Summaries should include the problem and the steps people took to overcome it.

Write About It

Discuss your writing with your instructor.

## Unit 7 Review

**Page 99**

A. 1. camera
2. Many, street
3. together
4. photos

B. 1. bag *or* beat; bag
2. tag, tag
3. heat, heat
4. sag *or* seat; seat

C. 1. "We can help sell the food," said the children.

2. May said, "These are heavy bags of beets."

3. "You have to take a photo of the garden," said Reed.

## Final Review

**Page 102**

A. 1. tapes   2. give   3. video
4. see   5. fine   6. when

B. 1. tell, take, *or* tug; take
2. sell *or* sake; sell
3. nine; nine
4. make, mug, *or* mine; mine
5. rake *or* rug; rug

C. Discuss your sentences with your instructor.

**Page 103**

D. 1. children   2. upset   3. sometimes
4. people   5. downhill   6. leaves

E. 1. team   2. day   3. uniform
4. problem   5. need   6. there

119

Page 104

F. 1. hip, hope, hay, *or* heed; hope
   2. nip *or* need; need
   3. tip; tip
   4. cope; cope
   5. play; play

G. 1. "I can help you with this garden," said Will.
   2. Rose said, "You can carry this heavy load for me."
   3. "No problem," said Will.

H. 1. He is a <u>helper</u>, a <u>reader</u>, and a good <u>worker</u>.
   2. Yes, he is a <u>player</u> on our team.
   3. He stopped being a <u>smoker</u> on June 8, 2000.

Page 105

I. 1. together
   2. carry, truck
   3. drive
   4. team, right *or* together
   5. teach

J. 1. cute *or* cold; cute
   2. June; June
   3. tight, tune, *or* told; told
   4. night; night
   5. big *or* bold; big

K. 1. The camera is in the (bag, sag).
   2. Nothing can (neat, beat) a good photo!
   3. Take a (heat, seat) right there.
   4. I will (wag, nag) you to sit still.

# Learner Checklist  Reading for Today  Book Three

| Skill | Completion | Skill | Completion | Skill | Completion |
|---|---|---|---|---|---|

## Unit 1
Review Words ......................... ☐
Sight Words ............................ ☐
Phonics: Short *e* (-ell) ............. ☐
Phonics: Long *a* (-ake) ........... ☐
Writing Skills: Compound
    Words .............................. ☐
Comprehension ..................... ☐
Unit 1 Review ....................... ☐

## Unit 2
Review Words ......................... ☐
Sight Words ............................ ☐
Phonics: Short *u* (-ug) ............ ☐
Phonics: Long *i* (-ine) ............. ☐
Writing Skills: Irregular
    Plurals .............................. ☐
Comprehension ..................... ☐
Unit 2 Review ....................... ☐

## Unit 3
Review Words ......................... ☐
Sight Words ............................ ☐
Phonics: Short *i* (-ip) .............. ☐
Phonics: Long *o* (-ope) ........... ☐
Writing Skills: Adding -*er*
    to Naming Words ............... ☐
Comprehension ..................... ☐
Unit 3 Review ....................... ☐

## Unit 4
Review Words ......................... ☐
Sight Words ............................ ☐
Phonics: Long *a* (-ay) ............. ☐
Phonics: Long *e* (-eed) ........... ☐
Writing Skills: Using
    Commas ........................... ☐
Comprehension ..................... ☐
Unit 4 Review ....................... ☐

## Unit 5
Review Words ......................... ☐
Sight Words ............................ ☐
Phonics: Long *i* (-ight) ............ ☐
Phonics: Long *u*
    (-une, -ute) ...................... ☐
Writing Skills: Irregular
    Verbs ............................... ☐
Comprehension ..................... ☐
Unit 5 Review ....................... ☐

## Unit 6
Review Words ......................... ☐
Sight Words ............................ ☐
Phonics: Short *i* (-ig) .............. ☐
Phonics: Long *o* (-old) ............ ☐
Writing Skills: Dropping
    Final -*e* to Add -*ed*
    and -*ing* ......................... ☐
Comprehension ..................... ☐
Unit 6 Review ....................... ☐

## Unit 7
Review Words ......................... ☐
Sight Words ............................ ☐
Phonics: Short *a* (-ag) ............ ☐
Phonics: Long *e* (-eat) ........... ☐
Writing Skills: Quotation
    Marks ............................... ☐
Comprehension ..................... ☐
Unit 7 Review ....................... ☐

Final Review .......................... ☐

# Word List

Below is a list of the 195 words that are presented to students in Book Three of *Reading for Today*. These words are introduced on sight word, phonics, and writing skills language pages. The words will be reviewed in later books. Students should also be familiar with other words based on the phonetically regular spellings of long and short vowel sounds in the consonant-vowel-consonant (CVC) and consonant-vowel-consonant + silent e (CVC+ e) patterns.

**A**
action

**B**
bag
bake
baseball
beat
because
bell
bold
bug
buyer

**C**
came
camera
carry
child
clay
clinic
clip
cold
come
cope
cute

**D**
day
deed
Dell
different
dig
dine
dip
disabled
doctor
does
down
downhill
drag
drive
dug
dune

**F**
fake
faked
faking
feat
feed
fell
fig
fight
fine
fold

**G**
gag
game
gave
give
gold

**H**
hay
heat
heavy
heed
helper
hip
hold
hope
hoped
hoping
hug

**J**
Jay
jug
June

**L**
lag
lake
lay
learn
leaves
life
liked
liking
line
lip
lives
lonely
lope
loved
loving
lug
lute

**M**
make
many
may
meat
men
might
mind
mine
mold
mope
more
mug
mute

**N**
nag
neat
need
Nell
night
nip

**O**
outlet
own

**P**
parents
person
photo
pig
pine
player
prison
problem
prune

**R**
rag
rake
ray
reader
records
reed
rig
right
rip
road
rope
rug

**S**
sag
said
sake
say
seat
see
seed
sell
shake
shell
shine
ship
shop
sight
sip
smoker
social worker
sold
sometimes
still
street

**T**
tag
take
talker
tapes
teach
team
tell
there
these
things
tight
time
timed
timing
tip
together
told
took
treat
truck
tug
tune
tuned
tuning

**U**
uniform
used
using

**V**
value
video
videotape
vine

**W**
wag
wake
want
way
weed
were
what
wheat
when
whine
who
wig
wine
women
worker
workout

**Z**
zip